THE NECESSARY EARTH

THE NECESSARY EARTH

nature and solitude in American literature

by WILSON O. CLOUGH

UNIVERSITY OF TEXAS PRESS • AUSTIN

MIDDLEBURY COLLEGE LIBRARY

PS
163
C6

6/1965
Am. Lit.

Library of Congress Catalog Card No. 64–13314
Copyright © 1964 by Wilson O. Clough
All Rights Reserved

PUBLISHED WITH THE ASSISTANCE OF A GRANT
FROM THE FORD FOUNDATION
UNDER ITS PROGRAM FOR THE SUPPORT OF PUBLICATIONS
IN THE HUMANITIES AND SOCIAL SCIENCES

Manufactured in the United States of America

TO LAURA

In Memoriam

PREFACE

This little book is offered more as an essay than as an exercise in research scholarship. That is, it arose from a desire to explore the broader features of a topic that is both difficult to make precise and indefinite in its outlines. It is an investigation of but one of many facets within the American experience, and that in its major outlines only; yet the task is approached with confidence in the validity of its claim to a hearing within the larger story. As is customary in writing an essay, more attention was given to identifying quotations that came readily to mind than to compiling notecards on the work of others, and more thought expended on the possibility of insights into the general topic and the original sources than to the routines of academic investigation. That there are certain risks in this method is obvious; but long habitation in academic halls has provoked the wish to reflect on one's own for a change.

The actual incentive came from a request to prepare, upon somewhat short notice, three public lectures in the summer of 1960, as a part of the William Robertson Coe Summer Conference in American Studies at the University of Wyoming. This book retains in its three major divisions the titles of those lectures, though they have all been measurably expanded here, and within them have been incorporated two articles elsewhere published and properly acknowledged below. The series of lectures was originally entitled "Nature and Solitude in American Literature."

These three divisions consider in sequence: first, the initial impact of the New World upon Old World men and the beginnings of the American experience; second, the gradual awareness that the frontier might furnish American writers with a native source of metaphor and analogy fruitful in the search for a national expression; and third, the degree to which echoes of this native metaphor and concentration may have lingered into the twentieth century.

Since I have elsewhere [1] investigated in some degree the intellectual antecedents of the founding fathers and the great body of classical and Western European literature that lay behind the resolutions of the new Republic, I cannot be accused of an undue bias in favor of the native note alone. Nevertheless, I have here wished to approach the American theme from the other side, that of the simple, often unlettered, American, not of the elite, and progressively divorced from that European heritage as he moved westward to test by daily acquaintance the hard, empirical facts of an untamed nature and its inevitable solitudes. He it was who experienced most of American history, and from his ranks rose more than one national figure. What effect, then, had that experience upon a national psychology, and eventually upon a native literature, for better or for worse, even if that literature could come only with increased literacy and upon the older Atlantic coast?

In the consideration of this query, two words are to be kept in mind throughout: *experience,* the emphasis upon the native experience as generative beyond the contributions of cultural inheritance and foreign influence; and *metaphor,* a basic element in all imaginative activity and, as drawn from the American experience, regarded as a source, in terms of literary and poetic expression, of much that we may call our own.

It may be that this native theme can be exaggerated as to its importance; or that this study, taken by itself, suggests a disproportionate emphasis upon its dynamism; or again, that, though once present, this theme is now all but irrelevant. That may be so. Nevertheless, the central problem for a native literature, as for a native political health, has always been: Can the average man speak meaningfully for himself and from his own experience and judgment? Can he be trusted (by whom? one may ask) to refer to his own experience and judgment

---

[1] Wilson O. Clough (ed.), *Intellectual Origins of American National Thought: Pages from the Books Our Founding Fathers Read.*

without undue reverence for the codified and entrenched judgment and experience and tradition of other lands and other times? The frontier experience suggested that he assume such independence or perish in that raw environment. Even so, could he carry over his hard-earned self-reliance into other areas, or must government and literature remain forever the property reserved for a sophistication denied to the many?

To phrase such a question opens up certain tantalizing possibilities within the American story. For example, in American literature the common man, though himself largely without literary voice, had to remain a central fact. The American writer, being writer, had to keep in touch with this source—this simple, democratic man—and at the same time, extend himself to consider the larger implications for self, for the American, for mankind. Here, indeed, we may discern a dominant American necessity, whether tacitly accepted or overtly rejected.

The political thesis lingers with us, as witness the charter of the United Nations. The literary form the theme takes may be of several sorts: it may be merely the popular stock response to "frontier" words as prestige words; it may be the later nostalgia of a Sandburg, a Thomas Wolfe, or a Faulkner, which is to say, with overtones of misgivings; it may be the acceptance of defeat, as in Robinson Jeffers' grim phrase, America's "heavily thickening to empire"; or it may appear in unexpected phrasings and forms in a John Dewey, a Wallace Stevens, or even a foreign observer.

There can, thus, be no hard and fast answer to our query. Men neglect at their own risk the memory and the disciplines of the past; yet they also continue to rise often from the humblest circumstances to challenge, as individuals, the finality of their exclusion from entrenched patterns. Though the American progressively lost much of the heritage of the past, he *could* speak with authority and personal confidence upon his own experience; and from that source he could draw analogies in areas other than the purely geographical and industrial, areas more customarily reserved to the voices of ancient tradition and habitual authority. This indifference to the fixed and final has always been the challenge of the New World man, and it continues to disturb when it speaks out freely.

We shall explore in somewhat outline fashion, then, such queries as those above, rephrased for our purpose as follows: Did the experience of the earlier American upon the frontiers of nature and solitude, a frontier stretching from the initial Atlantic foothold to the far shores of the Pacific, enter in any demonstrable way into the thinking and the literature of this country? The argument here is that it did—if only because all art, science, and philosophy must return at intervals, however unwillingly, to the base: the experience of the individual and the race, within whatever is.

One further point may be clarified. The writer, whatever he may say upon the Far Western theme, has not been concerned to evaluate that scene as such but only to fit it into the larger query. There is a rich and growing literature of Westerniana and a special enthusiasm for its promotion, with excellent Western presses and collections for the specialist. This essay aims at a more national theme.

The fact that a writer is deeply indebted to the reading of many years is sometimes but another way of saying that it is difficult for the literary scholar to free himself from the inhibitions of a cautious discipline, or to write with the directness and confidence of the real writers about whom he writes. This is a problem not sufficiently considered in the psychology of literary creativity, particularly in a day when literature tends to seek a haven in academic halls from the hazards of a complete devotion to its own art.

I wish to thank particularly Dr. T. A. Larson, director of the American Studies program at the University of Wyoming, for his encouragement toward my development of the original three lectures upon which this essay is based.

WILSON O. CLOUGH

Laramie, Wyoming

PERMISSIONS

For permission to quote certain copyrighted materials, I thank the following:

Alfred A. Knopf, Inc.
Stephen Crane, *Collected Poems*, 1951; and *Twenty Stories*, 1940.
Wallace Stevens, *The Collected Poems of Wallace Stevens*, 1957; *The Necessary Angel*, 1951; and *Opus Posthumous*, 1957.

Random House, Inc.
Robinson Jeffers, "The Eye," *The Double Axe and Other Poems*. Copyright 1948 by Robinson Jeffers. Reprinted from *The Double Axe and Other Poems*, by Robinson Jeffers, by permission of Random House, Inc.
———, "Life from the Lifeless," *Solstice and Other Poems*. Copyright 1935 and renewed 1962 by Donnan Jeffers and Garth Jeffers. Reprinted from *The Selected Poetry of Robinson Jeffers*, by permission of Random House, Inc.
———, "Gale in April," *Roan Stallion, Tamar, and Other Poems*. "Gale in April," copyright 1924 and renewed 1951 by Robinson Jeffers. Reprinted from *Roan Stallion, Tamar, and Other Poems*, by Robinson Jeffers, by permission of Random House, Inc.
———, "Fire on the Hills," *Thurso's Landing, Dear Judas, and Other Poems*. Copyright 1932 and renewed 1959 by Robinson Jeffers. Reprinted from *The Selected Poetry of Robinson Jeffers*, by permission of Random House, Inc.
———, "Science," "Shine, Perishing Republic," "Night," "Boats in a Fog," *Roan Stallion, Tamar, and Other Poems*. "Science," "Shine Perishing Republic," "Night," "Boats in a Fog," copyright 1925 and renewed 1953 by Robinson Jeffers. Reprinted from *The Selected Poetry of Robinson Jeffers*, by permission of Random House, Inc.

William Faulkner, "The Bear," *Go Down, Moses and Other Stories.* "The Bear," copyright 1942 by The Curtis Publishing Co. Copyright 1942 by William Faulkner. Reprinted from *Go Down, Moses and Other Stories,* by William Faulkner, by permission of Random House, Inc.

Charles Scribner's Sons
Thomas Wolfe, *From Death to Morning,* 1935; and *Of Time and the River,* 1935.

Alan Swallow, Publisher
Allen Tate, *Collected Essays,* 1959.

Thomas Hornsby Ferril
New and Selected Poems (Harper Brothers, 1952). Reprinted by permission of Thomas Hornsby Ferril.

Holt, Rinehart and Winston, Inc.
Robert Frost, "A Cabin in the Clearing," from *In the Clearing.* Copyright 1951, (c) 1962 by Robert Frost. Reprinted by permission of Holt, Rinehart and Winston, Inc.
———, *Complete Poems of Robert Frost.* Copyright 1923, 1934, 1947 by Holt, Rinehart and Winston, Inc. Copyright 1936 by Robert Frost. Copyright renewed 1951, (c) 1962 by Robert Frost. Copyright renewed (c) 1964 by Lesley Frost Ballantine. Reprinted by permission of Holt, Rinehart and Winston, Inc.

Chapters IV ("Nature at Bay") and XII ("Not from Landscape, Not from Flight"), here slightly revised, have been reprinted by editorial permission from, respectively, *The Texas Quarterly,* V (Autumn, 1962), and Union College *Symposium,* I (Spring, 1962).

Further acknowledgments of sources appear in the footnotes and in a brief Bibliography.

W. O. C.

CONTENTS

THE NECESSARY EARTH

There is a human loneliness,
A part of space and solitude,
In which knowledge cannot be denied.

—Wallace Stevens, "The Sail of Ulysses"

part 1   THE SHOCK OF GEOGRAPHY

Be free, all worthy spirits, and stretch yourselves.

—George Chapman, *Byron's Conspiracy*

i. Prologue

SOMETHING NEW began with the discovery of America. Perhaps nothing so startling to Western Europe can happen again as that first awareness that two vast and hitherto unknown continents lay to the west on a suddenly enlarged and now definitely global world—nothing, that is, until some far-roving adventurer touches a distant planet and returns with his first observations. And even then that discovery would be but a projection of an age of marvels that opened with the two Americas.

Legends of the past gave way to a stirring present reality, though that reality remained for a time shrouded in the half mythical; and the reality began its own accumulation of the legendary, though the new legends were of a different order, rooted this time in experience, not on the lost horizons of myth.

At first the European man tried desperately to link the lineaments of the new reality with past myths, or the myths with the reality; but in time the reality was sufficient to itself, and wonder was available within a real world. Thus a new kind of man arose for whom the reality was more important than the preservation of old myths. Myths lost their sharper outlines and began to fade—are

fading still, for we live, in a sense, in a very present world. Even
the newest excursions into space are performed less and less in the
expectation of coming upon monstrous apparitions and legendary
beings, but in the calmness of an insistence on knowing the exact
nature of the experiential universe in which we find ourselves—a
universe awful enough in its vastness and its immeasurable reaches
to tempt and test the creative and orderly imagination beyond all
past experiences, but tempting in the name of knowing and seeing
with utmost clarity.

In the shaping of this new mind of man, the discovery of America
played an important part from the beginning, the more so as its
pragmatic spirit turned first to reshaping the political environment
toward a greater freedom for all men and then to the practical
application of its knowledge to relieve men of their heaviest labors
by a command over the resources of nature. This was a new kind of
humanism, unknown to the ancient Greeks or to the Renaissance,
much as they contributed to the change of opinion; and it affected
the very springs of men's behavior in human society. Today the
world faces a dramatic choice: old rivalries, or a new kind of feder-
ated world which will borrow lessons from the American compromises with diversity and the American emphasis on individual
freedom and the open society.

The knowledge of that New World shook the Old World
mightily, and it would never be the same again. Fragments of the
older, more circumscribed world exploded into national rivalries,
colonizing ambitions, dreams of cities of gold and cities of Zion,
Utopias practical and Utopias visionary, explorations physical and,
not least, explorations intellectual and moral.

The Golden Age of a vanished past shifted to a new surge of
hope for an earthly future. "Be free, all worthy spirits, and stretch
yourselves,"[1] urged the Elizabethan poet and dramatist George

[1] George Chapman, *Byron's Conspiracy*, III, iii (1608).

Chapman; and Francis Bacon in his *Novum Organum* more soberly, observed: "It would, indeed, be dishonourable to mankind, if the regions of the material globe, the earth, the sea, the stars, should be so prodigiously developed and illustrated in our age, and yet the boundaries of the intellectual globe should be confined to the narrow discoveries of the ancients." Here are the two themes: freedom for the human spirit, and a stretching of the boundaries of human knowledge.

But while this dramatic change, European as much as American, was impending, simple, separate human individuals were increasingly experiencing at first hand what it was to advance alone into unmapped nature and to encounter in its solitudes a new discipline, the discipline of self-reliance and dependence on self. The actualities of first settlement, that is, were far from easy. Hunger, want, and fear were the lot of many, and the vast and lonely reaches of the land ahead. The early records are full of both the new promise and the harsher fact of hardships. Nature was no kinder because the Atlantic had been crossed—was, indeed, harder, because without the comforting mementoes of the past.

Thus, as Europeans left their own shores and launched on the new adventure, they were inevitably changed by the impact of the actualities of survival. They became, for better or for worse, a new kind of man, new men, men thrown back on themselves, forced to choose between new alternatives. How thoroughly, then, did this newness of experience, this shock of enforced self-decision, this prolonged acquaintance with a vast, impersonal nature and the loneliness of endless forests and far-lying plains, enter into the psychology and the literature of the Americans to be?

It is not a sufficient answer to join in the popular chorus of enthusiasm for the "old frontier" and its rawer episodes; nor, on the other hand, can we dismiss the experience as but a passing phase of settlement, after which the American moves to rejoin the old European procession.

D. H. Lawrence, in that odd and provocative book, *Studies in Classic American Literature,* because he writes as a European, only partially sees the fact when he writes: "Somewhere deep in every American heart lies a rebellion against the old parenthood of Europe. Yet no American feels he has completely escaped its mastery. Hence the slow, smouldering patience of the American opposition. The slow, smouldering corrosive obedience to the old master Europe, the unwilling subject." [2] Rebellion there has been; but the deeper note is elsewhere, less opposition than the cumulative habit of attachment to one's own experience. Indeed, today one might almost, if it were not unfair, question both syntax and allocation in that last phrase, "the unwilling subject."

What does lie deep in many an American heart is a curious kind of "mystique" in response to the reaches of his own land, an irrational, emotional surge of feeling peculiarly evident in the American and Canadian west, where nature must long linger in an austere remoteness. And herein, perhaps, lies a clue to our search. The American's attachment is often less to history, even his own, than to the memory of a conquest, yet a defeat, in the spaces of his own west, and the sentiment that these geographical symbols arouse of a still untamed remoteness from and indifference to man's little cries for a special consideration in his universe.

Such a statement may be unwarranted by the present scene; yet no one who has dwelt in the six or eight states dominated by the continental divide can fail to know this deeply rooted attachment to the open spaces. It is the residue of a portion of national history that bit deep into the popular consciousness. Often it takes on sentimental overtones: all that is associated with the Old West is affectionately denominated "old" with complete disregard of its recentness—the old trapper, the old mountain man, Indian scout, pioneer rancher, cowboy, gunman. And even the more sophisticated American, as he flies over the gaunt landscapes of the desert states, or

[2] D. H. Lawrence, *Studies in Classic American Literature,* pp. 6–7.

scales the peaks of the Rockies, or cruises in his car across the vast
plains and mountain heights from Canada to the Mexican border,
may confess to a kind of inner gratitude for these uninhabited and
uninhabitable stretches that the eye cannot encompass in any one
glance.

What is this compelling pull of nature untamed? Is it genuine,
indigenous, native; or is it manufactured and synthetic? Is it limited
to the unsophisticated? Obviously not. Or has it bitten deeper into
the national consciousness and touched even the body of literature
which we call American letters, especially the novel, the poem,
the literary essay?

The problem is not an easy one, since the evidence must lie, in
its initial terms, not in libraries and doctoral theses but in the knowledge and the feelings of men and women not themselves given to
literary expression. In time, perhaps, the communal sense will find
literary expression. It is never amiss, therefore, to consider how
place and experience may have furnished subject matter, and, more
deeply, how they may have suggested simile and metaphor, those
indicators of the writer's way of envisioning his material and also
of the degree to which he may have departed from the more formal
inheritance. Literature is everywhere a compound of time, place,
and the individual projection of personal experience and reflection
into objective forms, forms in part determined by the writer's
heritage but, also, if he is more than plagiarist, in part created out
of his own living and experience and his own inner compulsions.

Such an observation is peculiarly apt for the American in view
of the native experience with newness, the three centuries of
response to the western lure, and the great number of writers who,
apart from the New England school, have lacked formal education
beyond the elementary levels. Even the New England school
wavered between respect for the British models and the possibilities
that lay within the native theme. When we read that British critics,
for example, were puzzled in the 1850's to account for so richly

endowed a book as *Moby-Dick* from a "mere sailor," we should reflect less on British complacency than on this same unlikely product from the unconventional preparation, and on the American compulsion to communicate the native experience and difference. That any man, especially one like Melville or Whitman, arising from the ranks, should feel compelled to examine his heritage in his own uninhibited terms, is the best of indicators that a native literature will arrive. A Melville, a Whitman, a Mark Twain, whose formal schooling reached barely into the teens, may, even at his worst, say more about the mood and mind of his countrymen than all the incidental parallels with European literature would ever discover. And who can assert confidently when a man may have borrowed or may have forged his own way through personal experience to a similar, or perhaps a contrary, conclusion? Such is the way of science and its expectation of the confirmation of others working independently. Such is the way of living literature.

There are, therefore, certain obvious difficulties in approaching our theme. Anyone who looks in a library for studies of nature in American literature will find little beyond a few old-fashioned tracts written in the spirit of awe toward the works of the Creator, with illustrations from the minor poets, or incidental mention of nature in studies of the romantic movement in American literature. This study is primarily neither of these, though not unrelated.

Again the term "man in nature" suggests to others the national heritage of the frontier legend. There is, of course, a very considerable body of work on the frontier as a special theme, and on the other hand an impressive growth in American scholarship dealing with our literary heritage, now rapidly expanding into a European interest in the same topic. An older tendency in studies of American literature was to give particular attention to how American literature might be related by source and parallel to its European antecedents, particularly the British. More recently, newer techniques of analysis in depth, and the application of special criteria—psychological, psychoanalytical, sociological or semantic—have added a host of stimulating books to our shelves.

Yet between the deeply American saga of the frontier, its explorers, mountain men, or cowboys, and the realm of major American letters, there appears to lie a kind of cultural no man's land. It is the realm of average folk, whose history includes neither western drama nor eastern scholarship, and whose powers of self-expression are neither developed nor vocal, yet whose massive impact is upon every political election, every defeat of special privilege, every poet or novelist hailed as a native voice.

Must there be this gap in understanding, this divergence of stream? Or might we find that the long native experience with frontier or farm, forest or sea, crude as it was in parlor or library terms, has still made itself felt in some appreciable strength in our major literary expression, either to modify its course or to introduce some element not available within the mind and habit of Europe? At times, the assumption has appeared to be that the only road to an American literature was that of a rejection of its native crudities and an anxious search for some lost European psyche, or of exhortations to consider what it is to be a cultivated European. The answer is not to be found in any crude chauvinism, nor yet in a rejection of the great heritage of the European past, but in a simple adherence to a central American principle: the right to bring each before the bar of the American experience. The semantics of the problem is that of expression seeking new resources in an older vocabulary or, if need be, a new vocabulary of its own.

The specialist on the frontier theme has, in effect, often been treated as if he were slightly subliterary, an attitude unfortunately sometimes justified by an excess or a narrowness, even a partisanship, in his enthusiasms. The specialist in European, especially British, literature, on the other hand, has been accorded the respect due to sanctioned scholarship, since he must write with an eye to other

scholars thoroughly equipped with an arsenal of critical and biblio-
graphical weapons. Indeed, only since the turn of the century has
the student of American letters been conceded a reasonably comparable position in the hierarchy of scholarly studies.

There have, of course, been good reasons for the delay, now no
longer serious, in American studies. Yet, moving about among the
"scholars" in the various "disciplines," one comes finally to suspect
that below the urbane surfaces there still exists the old dichotomy
of Gilbert and Sullivan's conserva-tive and liber-al, of Platonist and
Aristotelian, of right wing and left, of empiricist and idealist, of
frontiersman and urbanite. It is not necessary to insist that such
categories are hard and fast nor that they are immediately applicable
to all, but simply that what is native in the American product may
or may not attract the scholar.

Thus, when the professor of English speaks somewhat condescend-
ingly of American letters as lacking, as it were, the traditional, the
systematic categories and the philosophic pigeonholes that count so
heavily in European scholarship, when he looks upon Emerson,
Hawthorne, Whitman, even Henry James, as at best fairly interesting amateurs but something short of Europe's own, he is uncon-
sciously assuming that the hallowed categories are sufficient to encompass the total American experience; and, worse, he is ignoring
the central problem of the American writer, which is to speak from
his own experience and knowledge.

Ever since Jamestown and Plymouth, if not even earlier, the
major fact of the New World has been its shock to Old World
perspectives and complacencies, the impossibility of fitting the new
experience neatly and without disruption into the Old World habits.
The result has been too often the artificial assumption that one
must choose between the relatively fixed norms of the past or a
kind of perverse rejection of cultural standards. Yet there had to be
an interim of shifting values as well as the element of selectivity
among the settlers. Those first European emigrants, it should be

obvious, transplanted themselves, names, institutions, beliefs, as Europeans. Even their religious dissent, even their lower-class resentments toward the past, were European bred and European determined, though at the same time they made their contribution to the prevailing American temper of dissent. What happened afterward, however, was the work of a vast, uncompromising landscape which made no concessions to preconceptions, indeed, implacably compelled one concession after another, until old connotations no longer held and new habits became grounded in self-reliance and reference to one's own judgment and experience, since no other criteria were available or pertinent, or, at best, those that were had to be adapted to new conditions.

Today, as we move with increasing speed from that past, even our own, like Melville's Ishmael, with a sense of "rushing from all havens astern," we may wonder if history itself is not deserting us, and leaving us no knowledge but the immediate experience. Yet that simpler past is still a part of the basic pattern, worthy as such of a moment's glance.

Two reasons, then, have already been suggested for the neglect of our own simpler story. The first of these is the difficulty of getting at the mid-area of the folk without a literary voice, the inarticulate who have learned to survive without the relief of sophisticated expression, whose language and whose minds are filled with clichés, popular generalizations, stock responses, the simpler habits of the daily routine. They comprehend little of the intricate subtleties of our avant-garde magazines and books. They never did; and when the scholar completes his abstruse examination of Puritanism, for example, the fact remains, as Perry Miller has recognized, that 90 per cent of the Puritans were still average English small-town folk with very little to distinguish them from those they left behind them.

Our earliest settlers were neither Shakespeares nor Miltons, neither Jacob Boehmes nor Isaac Newtons. Whether the dominating motive for colonization was economic opportunism or religious separatism or sheer escape from an unpromising and stultifying lot, the colonists were drawn chiefly from the lower ranks within the European hierarchies, and came with no expectation of aping the aristocracies of art or literature. Indeed, they brought with them many of the same social distinctions they had left behind, and again it was the necessities of the frontier that weakened and scattered these distinctions.

The second reason already hinted at is the semantic one. Literature in any society is a thing of slow maturation and is never notable in colonies in their primary stages. Yet when it does finally appear, its liveliest claim to attention is to have arisen from within the new experience, not from a sedulous duplication of the old. If to have humble ancestors, drawn from the underprivileged of Europe, were to be doomed to a static incapacity, then, obviously, American faith in the human potential would be a bit of romantic folly. The evidence is before us, however, that talent, like gold in the far west, is where you find it; or, like transplanted plants, it may wither or flourish according to the environmental prospect.

More to our purpose, however, is the fact that words must have failed these early observers, for the old words did not always jibe with the new experience. The pages of the first explorers, for example, have about them the strangeness of lands unknown to us today. That strangeness lies in part in the inadequacies of their vocabulary. Not only did plain objects have to be identified and named, but new emotions strained old formulas. In place of the familiar connotations of the Old World, new ones had to be forged, new terms invented, even Indian sounds adapted. Literature lives by powerful connotations, but these must be appropriate, and they must be cumulative, built out of repeated experiences, shared by others.

A third factor appears in the isolation of the New World man, the removal from familiar scenes, from old villages and old friends, from schools and books and materials for writing. However sharp and novel the first visual impressions, much was inevitably sacrificed in the delay of establishing oneself against sheer starvation and threats to life, until such daily pressures dulled the edges of expression. Men became taciturn and sparing of speech, losing much of the old resources of fluent, poetic, and literary language. Such taciturnity was reinforced on the frontiers by the need not to scare game, not to provoke ambush, not to expose self and others to danger and death. And the deep forests, the gloom of rocks and silent ranges, the soundless shadows and the inhospitable solitudes—for North America was one solid forest from Hudson Bay to Florida, and but sparsely inhabited by the red man—must have made their impression and exacted their toll. Something of these experiences emerges in the forest scenes of Cooper, the captivity records, the wooded hills of Bryant, the gloom of Hawthorne, even the brighter pages of Thoreau, though lightened there by the fields and pastures of a longer habitation.

Add to this sparseness of words the Puritan preference for uncompromising speech without the frosting of rhetoric, the Quaker plainness of speech and its emphasis on the inner experience, the general apartness of human beings everywhere beyond the first settlements, and, as mentioned, the universal preoccupation with the material necessities, and we shall hardly be surprised at the belated appearance of anything like a formal literature. The New England settlers, perhaps more than any others, fought this threat to a transplanted culture by a tighter township organization, immediate provision for education of the young, and a theocratic control; yet their complaints against the obstacles of free land and human perversity are easy to find.

But there is for the student of literary culture a deeper consideration. All effective literary expression moves from imagery to verbal form. Without this transfer, and in this direction, there is no vigorous literature. The problem for literature, even in a favorable climate, is to freshen old language, not to repeat it interminably but to present the familiar in new and challenging ways. "To make you *see*"—that is the desperate cry of every dedicated artist; but by what means? The way is prescribed—that of a return to the original, initiating experience. In a new environment the problem is no less acute: it is to present the new so as to make it familiar, to create, that is, directly from experience. This emphasis should be kept in mind; it has a profound relevancy to our whole thesis.

We perceive, then, a new reason why the man on the frontier, deprived of the more obvious advantages of a cultural environment, suffers a double burden if he would be literary. He not only lacks the approved disciplines of the past—this his critics will never let us forget—but he is further confronted by a unique problem, that of inventing a new language for a new need. Therefore, thrust into an older, sophisticated society, he is likely to become diffident, ill at ease, especially with words. What he knows he finds it hard to express, for he senses that the word associations are not his. Not until a Mark Twain appears will he find a spokesman indifferent to convention and free with the colloquial language; and even Twain will know his moments of deepest doubt. For even when the man from the frontiers of culture knows, is inwardly sure, that his own answers serve him better in his own environment, he may hesitate before the patronizing doubts of the assured, or be unable to assert himself in the face of established opinion and habit, the traditional, the formal. Given a certain training or compulsion, he may nevertheless make the effort. Fortunately for our political history, Adams, Jefferson, Madison, were not so handicapped, being inheritors on the frontier of a Renaissance and a classical tradition, educated in the language of their inheritance and not lacking in the needful terms, yet at the same time sufficiently American to refuse to be cowed by the past.

"Long must he stammer in his speech," said Emerson of the American scholar; for he had something new to say to the world, but he had yet to find the way to say it. Emerson had just advised the American scholar to turn from Old World traditions and seek out his own genius, his own certainties, to rely on himself and not to be dismayed if the world made noises in unison to the contrary. For the New World man, if ever there were or were to be this new and rising genius, this would be no light assignment. Americans, Emerson reasoned, had first to create a new language out of the common, daily experience, to find new subjects from a new world, fresh approaches, with analogies drawn from their own observations, and, for the first time in all history, to do all this with a genuine consideration for the meaning of the ordinary man. No wonder the New World scholar must stammer in his speech. He had not only to create a new language, to explore afresh a new and personal experience, but also to defy the pretense of finality in old customs and habits under which the common man had too long been treated as clown, slave, serf, oaf, servant, peasant automatically barred from the concerns of high literature. The challenge was indeed considerable.

There may be a further reason for the neglect of this mid-ground realm of a native experience. Scholarship today is almost of necessity directed at impressing itself and its pupils with the vast accumulations of new learning. From Plato to Sartre the revaluations of young scholars flood upon us; and bright young men, mostly urban in origin and increasingly out of touch or sympathy with a waning American past, feel it incumbent upon them to attack American letters in new terms—symbolism, the economic motive, existentialism, the fascinations of that new-old word, "myth," psychoanalysis, and the newer criticism. This present comment is not in the way of complaint, merely of observation. Nevertheless, stimulating and provocative as such exercises may be, the fact of American literature

up to and into the twentieth century has been simpler, nearer the
little village of Concord in pre–Civil War days or the looseness of
Virginia City in 1865.

American literature of the past has been most American precisely
when it has been least concerned to fit some transplanted formula,
most American when it has consulted first its own observation and
its own experience. This is simply a statement of fact. If American
literature has been in its course more naive, less deserving, than
that of some older society, we shall not falsify its character for all
that. The elaborate analyses of our own day of these older writers
leave us wondering if they would have understood more than a
fractional part of what is being said. Were they, then, childlike and
immature for not having these modern techniques at hand; if so,
what then makes them worthy of such elaborate scrutiny and
diagnosis? "Western," as applied to the total American experience,
must come to mean something more, it is true, than the raw frontier
and its practical exigencies, since these are but the physical and
overt elements. "Western" can come to spell a new effort and a new
opportunity to examine the past afresh, or to explore one's own
native insights; to undertake, in other words, the Emersonian task
of forging the new language and the new meaning. There is, in
such terms, a genuine difference between adopting some venerable
philosophy as the fixed yardstick for one's meditations, or reading
from one's own experience and reflection to a fresh insight on self,
on the art of living, even on the authors of the past and the modes
and manners of other lands and other times.

Sometimes this demanding effort toward a fresher view is known
as objectivity. Herbert Muller, wrestling in his *Uses of the Past*
with the problem of historical objectivity, concludes that objectivity
is possible only in free societies. It can never be tolerated in totali-
tarian states because objectivity, he argues, denotes an obligation to
begin with the concrete evidence and to allow conclusions and

systems to flow from that base. All repetition at second hand breeds a sense of inferiority, a willingness to submit to the judgment of others. Better to start with one's own, even if that act engender doubt and uncertainty, the risk of error, a sense of humility, even at first a lack of confidence in the self. Confidence will come, Emerson thought, with confirmations from the order of what is.

There is no intention here to assert the eternal rightness of American judgment or to deny the risks involved, but only to observe that the man in isolation, dependent on his own resources, will develop the habit and the preference. Emerson's insistence was the obverse of his own misgivings and doubts; and the awkwardness of the untutored man before the disciplined one is proverbial. One is reminded here, however, of an observation by George Santayana in his *Character and Opinion in the United States,* written in 1921. Americans, he observed, sometimes exhibit that "shyness which simple competence often shows in the presence of conventional shams." Their fresher insights, he added, may be "whispered in parentheses and asides"; yet he recognized, too, in them that "good old sense of curiosity about the nature of things," and even "an intense self-reliance; to exercise private judgment is not only a habit with them but a conscious duty." [3] They meet hoary systems, he commented, with a frank gaze; for, not being given to abstract speculation, they automatically apply the pragmatic test and seem not to recognize the right of any institution to coerce mind or conscience to the point of denying self-judgment.

This prologue, then, sums up a simple thesis, to be further explored by a search for the American at work upon his own experience. The insistence on self-reliance and the acknowledgment of the difficulties in the way are assumed to be based on a more native actuality than that of the Emersonian expression above. They are

---

[3] George Santayana, *Character and Opinion in the United States,* pp. 6, 145.

at once the source of an American diffidence in the past in the face of European accomplishments and the base for a national preference for consulting the evidence within and for oneself. Hence Emerson's awareness of the long stammering of the scholar to come, and the reason for his urgency in advancing the claims of self-reliance. Perhaps Emerson's intuition served him well.

ii. The Age of Wonder

PROPAGANDA began almost at once for the colonization of the New World. It took at first chiefly the form of an exaggeration of the riches and the opportunities that lay in wait for the taker. George Chapman, in a play with Marston (*Eastward Ho*, 1605), voiced the advantages of Virginia through a character, Seagull. Gold more plentiful than copper at home, he announced, and "you shall live freely there, without sergeants, or courtiers, or intelligencers. . . . You may be a nobleman and never be a slave. . . . Besides, there we shall have no more law than conscience, and not too much of either." [1] Thus the spell of the frontier was at work even before Jamestown, and the call of new freedoms from old forms and patterns. No wonder a tavern frequenter, hearing the speech, explodes in the play: "Gods me! How far is it thither?" The basic impulses of men are everywhere alike, and America lay in the future as a place to be built on the foundation of a common response to a new prospect.

First observations upon settlement were of two sorts: the immense

[1] *Eastward Ho!*, III, iii, p. 499, in *The Plays of George Chapman*, ed. Thomas M. Parrott. See also note, p. 865.

and inexhaustible wealth of the New World, and the hardships of
first settlement. Bradford's record at Plymouth touched at once
upon the second:

They had now no friends to welcome them nor inns to entertain or re-
fresh their weather-beaten bodies, no houses or much less towns to re-
pair to, to seek for succour . . . . All things stand upon them with a
weatherbeaten face, and the whole country, full of woods and thickets,
represented a wild and savage hue. If they looked behind them, there
was the mighty ocean which they had passed and was now as a main
bar and gulf to separate them from all the civil parts of the world.[2]

The solitudes of an untried geography enveloped them and imposed
upon them the first harsh hazards of a new self-dependence. Such
became the oft repeated lesson of a new continent to these men and
women who had cut their ties with the past and had launched frail
enterprises into the unknown and the unexplored, risking that
first-hand experience without sure precedents to guide them. It was
a challenge to strong men, a terror to the weak. Here were no cities,
no courts or mansions of the titled, no cathedrals, no royal, ecclesiastical, or military pomp, no humble streets, no homely farms or
familiar landmarks, no councillors or guardians, only the remoteness of tiny cabins beneath the looming, darksome forest, the isolation of tiny wooden hamlets, the long winters that bred introspection, loneliness, and silence.

Thus the American began as a seeker and a groper, physically
and spiritually, rejecting the past for a new hope, erecting his own
signposts, naming animals and plants, learning the ancient guidance
of the stars, the moss on trees, the flow of streams, the habits of
animals, the reflections of his own solitary living. In time this mode
of life became a habit, a resentment of being crowded or ordered, a
rejection of even his own transplanted governors, a boast, a lure,
a beacon lit by the western hills and the skies always beyond. Buried

[2] William Bradford, *Of Plimouth Plantation*, ed. S. E. Morison, pp. 61–62.

though this sentiment might be under the taciturnity of the frontiersman or within the material concentration of the rising Atlantic
settlements, it lay long under the surface of the American consciousness. It may be that this is the earliest and the most profoundly
rooted element in what is loosely labelled "the American way." It
lingers still in superficial folkways and artificial tourist-lures. It also
finds its way in more serious terms into the national literature.

The promises of the new horizons, however, outweighed for the
hardy the labors of beginning. Over and over again, the early
explorers, led on by the excitement of being the first to see, stress
the wonders of a new world, the apparently immeasurable wealth
of scenery, game, and rich lands, the abundance of flora and fauna,
the absence of human depredations, the possibilities awaiting the
bold settler. It was a land untouched by axe or plow, unexplored by
miner or huntsman or husbandman. The Indians were by and large
scattered, almost irrelevant in certain areas, and regarded by some
as a further curiosity, like the native animal life. It was a new Eden,
open for the takers, surpassing all expectations. People in Europe,
said the Frenchman Radisson, fight and take lives over a bare rock;
here is land untold, and most pleasant to see. So the reports accumulate, listing in glowing terms the countless wild birds, pigeons, ducks,
geese, herons, wild turkey; the deer, bear, bison, fish; the fruits,
wild grapes, berries, nuts; all in abundance.

There are few exceptions to this delight in abundance, even in
books that stress the hardships of winter travel or the scarcity of
needful supplies. Perhaps much of the enthusiasm has overtones of
propaganda for colonizing, as appears obvious, for example, in
George Alsop's *A Character of the Province of Maryland*, published
in England in 1666. "Neither do I think there is any place under
the Heavenly altitude," he writes, "or that has footing or room
upon the circular Globe of this world, that can parallel this fertile
and pleasant piece of ground in its multiplicity, or rather Nature['s]
extravagancy of a super-abounding plenty." Listing, like others,

the wealth of animal life, he turns to man's estate and promises relief for those who "are drove upon the Rocks of pinching wants." There are no beggars, no prisons, and "All Inquisitions, Martyrdoms, and Banishments are not so much as named." The lot of servants is light, and in the winter months they "do little or no work or imployment, save cutting of wood to make good fires to sit by"; that is, unless they wish to hunt "Deer or Bear . . . or Swans, Geese and Turkeys," all "most plentiful." Apprentices are soon free to set up as artisans or farmers themselves. Over-generous as Alsop's estimate may have been of his own four years in Maryland, his picture was not without foundation.[3]

John Smith, too, early lists the same wealth of fruits, woods of many sorts, birds, fish, and game in great abundance. Even William Bradford is inspired to step aside from his sermonizing and try rhyme, providing thereby concrete evidence that good and holy men are not necessarily endowed with poetic gifts:

> All sorts of roots and herbs in gardens grow,
> Parsnips, carrots, turnips, or what you'll sow,
> Onions, melons, cucumbers, radishes,
> Skirrets, beets, coleworts, and fair cabbages . . .
> Nuts and grapes of several sorts here are,
> If you will take the pains them to seek for.[4]

William Penn likewise reports at length to London in 1683 on fruits and game animals of the New World: "The White and Black Mulberry, Chestnut, Walnut, Plums, Strawberries, Cranberries, Hurtleberries and Grapes of divers sorts . . . Peaches, and very good, and in great quantities, not an Indian plantation without them . . ." And as to animals: "The Elk . . . , Deer bigger than ours, Beaver, Racoon, Rabbits, Squirrels, and some eat young

---

[3] See George Alsop in *Narratives of Early Maryland*, ed. Clayton C. Hall, pp. 344, 349, 357.

[4] The verses by Bradford are quoted in George F. Willison, *Saints and Sinners*, p. 339.

Bear . . . Turkey (forty and fifty pound weight) . . . Pheasants, Heath-birds, Pigeons and Partridges in abundance . . . Swan, Goose, white and gray, Brands, Ducks, Teal . . . nor so good have I ever eat in other countries . . ." [5] And so on. In similar vein Robert Beverly of Virginia raves over the "extream fruitfulness of that country." He gives two paragraphs to peaches, nectarines, and apricots alone; and as for hogs, they "swarm like vermine upon the earth." [6]

Such earthy attractions weighed mightily with the poor of Europe, especially since they seemed to be had for the asking and the effort. To the escapee from feudal tenantry, serfdom, military impressment, or a debtor's prison, they could be inducements indeed. They were not, of course, the sole sources of appeal. The common man of Europe had never had an easy lot, though no doubt better than that of Asia. Furthermore, in the sixteenth and seventeenth centuries, the nonconformist within a state religion, whether the prevailing opinion be Protestant or Catholic, risked accusations of treason and blasphemy, with consequent fines, whippings, confiscation of property if he had any, disenfranchisement and disqualifications of all sorts, even torture and death. "Flying the Depravations of Europe to the American strand," as Cotton Mather put it, the Puritan himself was none too gentle with dissenters from his creed; nevertheless, along with Quakers, Anabaptists, German Pietists, French Huguenots, and Maryland Catholics, he resisted with equal fervor a state church not his own, and took pains to keep before his colony its reason for coming, namely, to plant one or another new Zion, set upon a hill for all to remember. Eventually, yielding to diversities and the greater relaxations of the New World, their descendants would combine to abandon the whole principle of a state church.

[5] William Penn in "A Letter . . . to the Committee of the Free Society of Traders," London, 1683, *American Culture Series.*

[6] Robert Beverly, *History and Present State of Virginia, 1755,* ed. L. B. Wright, pp. 314–319.

There seems little doubt that the original Puritan in America thought of himself less as one cut off from English life than as a model for his English brethren, if not even for Europe itself. Still members within the Anglican fold, on their first coming, they wished to strengthen the resolution of their brethren at home, and to demonstrate how life might be lived, not on the remote frontier, but within the daily tasks of a mundane world. No doubt other religious groups shared the same hope of offering without interference the lesson of what it was to live as one ought. So the Quakers maintained for a long time a close contact with their English brethren; and even the Dutch Calvinists, though the Dutch colony was never a religious experiment in the New World, had until the Revolution no pastors or "dominies" who had not been educated in the Netherlands. Each hoped, however vaguely, to return one day in triumph to the homeland, if not actually at least by proxy, to exhibit the advantages of freedom from interference in the right to practice life as it should be lived at home.

Yet the New World compelled its concessions, and diversity prevailed over separation, even as forms yielded to simplicity. Already by 1677, Urian Oakes, viewing the Puritan defeat in England, advised his flock in New England to "labor to be prepared and provided for Disappointments."[7] Religion had linked them with Europe; the American continent progressively weakened the ties. As each group lost something of the original momentum under the shocks of hardship and the demands of a practical world over idealism, a rising younger generation without the original drive and familiar with the new land only, and the attrition of secular newcomers drawn by the demand for artisan and farmer and soon to outnumber the faithful, shifted attention to the New World and its imperative presence. Adjustments had to be made, and old tensions seemed of lesser importance.

[7] Urian Oakes, Conclusion to "The Sovereign Efficacy of Divine Providence," quoted in Perry Miller and T. N. Johnson, *The Puritans,* p. 367.

Yet the sense of a special mission need not be lost. It could be reinterpreted, or it might take new forms. Thus there entered into the American psychology a peculiar element, the sense of a special mission or, shall we say, special missions which blended gradually in a sense of a natural and a national mission, to show the world a new freedom, to exercise a special privilege of personal judgment on many things.

Whatever the manifold reasons, the American Revolutionary period was one of a low ebb of the old religious drive in its original terms, and yet at the same time a period of a widespread appeal to the common rights of man and the common belief in the natural foundations of morality and religion. This view is known loosely as deism, and it was held by most of the leading political figures of that era. It was not that religious leaders did not speak out— indeed, they were vocal to such a degree that some unfriendly observers blamed the Revolution on the clergy. But the voices on the American side more and more placed the new mission within the political frame and within the frame of individual rights.

Jonathan Mayhew, for example, in 1748, was most outspoken for a new liberty: "Nor has any man whatever, whether of a civil or sacred character, any authority to control us, unless it be by the gentle methods of argument and persuasion . . . Did I say, we have a *right* to judge and act for ourselves? I now add—it is our indispensable *duty* to do it." But, he added, "While we are asserting our own liberty and Christian rights, let us be consistent and uniform, and not attempt to incroach upon the rights of others."[8] Such words did no harm, at least, to the Revolutionary appeal for a new unity and a new mission to build on the rights of man.

Thus the Revolution, which is not our major topic here and will be summarily treated, obviously served to redirect the old sense of religious mission to a larger and more inclusive national mission

[8] Jonathan Mayhew, Sermon IV, "Objections Considered," which follows on Sermon III, "The Right and Duty of Private Judgment," in *Seven Sermons*, p. 86.

which could accommodate the old differences. There could be a new
unification of purpose and fervor, and a corrupt world could once
more be urged to look to America as the example set on a hill for
all to see, the example now of free men acting freely to form a
government according to their own wishes.

Examples of this transference would not be difficult to find, for it
was a common theme at the time—"the first people," said John
Jay, a sober and a religious man, "whom Heaven has favoured with
an opportunity of deliberating upon, and choosing the forms of
government under which they should live . . . under the guidance
of reason and experience." [9] Adams, Jefferson, Madison, James
Wilson, Franklin, many another, ring variations on this same tune.
Writers like Tom Paine, barely arrived in time to participate, repeat
it; and Philip Freneau, one of the first to respond in verse, prophesies
thus:

> Soldiers of Liberty,
> Disdain to bow the knee,
> But teach equality
>   To every shore.
> The world at last will join
> To aid thy grand design,
>   Dear Liberty.[10]

Thus the sense of mission and even divine destiny will reappear
in a new national pride, in communal experiments, social and
religious, in "Manifest Destiny," in a later "Make the world safe
for Democracy," even in a present uneasy sense of America's failure
to live up to its heritage of setting a corrupt world a better example.

On the frontiers of the new land such sentiments tend to fade
into a simple, sometimes even truculent, assertion of lawlessness,
though it is also true that Jeffersonianism finds its frontier counter-

---

[9] John Jay, "Charge . . . to the Grand Jury . . . in Ulster County, September 9,
1777," in *Early American Imprints, 1639–1800.*
[10] Philip Freneau, "Ode," in Harry H. Clark, *Major American Poets,* p. 54.

part and support, as witness the growth of a Lincoln. Again, a
Thoreau, product of the old New England environment, can feel
on the one hand a genuine pride in being American, and at the same
time reserve a Puritan right to rebuke his neighbors for not asserting
their own worth, their own right to dissent. The mission of America,
for him, was to arrive at an ideal stage in which the individual is
at last superior to government, is, indeed, government's reason for
being. This individual, obviously, cannot be the common run of
man; he would have to be, one might suppose, of a moral and social
order rare indeed. Nevertheless, "There will never be a really free
and enlightened State until the state comes to recognize the individual as a higher and independent power, from which all its own
power and authority are derived, and treats him accordingly." [11]
Perhaps the theme could go no further.

The links between Thoreau's ultimate demand on his country's
mission and the earlier Puritan right to dissent, separate, and withdraw in the name of a higher mission, or the Quaker's refusal to
heed any but the inner voice, or even the frontiersman's inherent
predilection for private judgment, might occupy us for some time.
Suffice it to say here that the natural setting of a New World with
an unlimited western horizon contributed not a little to make such
independency more than a fantasy.

Now a new query confronts the world—and history is made up of
questions put by new conditions and new actualities, and the answers
which men propose to them. The question may be put thus: "How
far can common, average man, released from the hallowed restraints,
traditional loyalties to king, court, army, church, social hierarchies,
even law, living almost as man in nature, be counted on to rise to
the new opportunities, the unchecked freedom? Will he not succumb to innate depravity and a Hobbesian brutishness? Dare he
assume a right solely in himself, without the tested sanctions, to life,

[11] Henry Thoreau, *Writings of Henry Thoreau,* concluding paragraph of "Civil
Disobedience."

liberty, and the pursuit of his own definition of what constitutes happiness?" The query is thoroughly legitimate, and the answers are still in the balance, for the examples that come to mind depend in part on the questioner's own preferences.

Many were the gloomy prophets. It was one thing for philosophers to toy with theories on the natural origin of society, theories Stoic and Epicurean in ancestry, as revived and elaborated since the Renaissance; but it was quite another thing for ordinary men in a present setting to put into practical application the assertion of an original right to review the original compact. We do not escape in any day the haunting suspicion of the human potential for depravity, the unreliability of man as man. But we need not force the American experiment into such extreme terms; for the men that moulded the new nation were all of them cautious men, staking more on an elaborate system of checks and balances against man's passion for power than on his innate goodness. The political answer was moderate, even if liberal and revolutionary, and its appeal was to reason and unimpassioned discussion.

Yet the setting in the New World was one to encourage an enthusiastic acceptance of the more revolutionary assertions. Such are the risks freedom must take. To assert that "man has no rights, only duties, or responsibilities, only obedience" is to assume the dictator's insolence. What is *his* right? It ends by being either that of brute power, against which the only answer is force, or that of some essentially mystical claim to a unique mission—today, under the international impact of the American experiment, the hollow pretense that he represents the people's will. The answer, it would appear, may range from a naive optimism to the more familiar contempt for man in the large. The thoughtful historian, more moderately conditioned, will recognize that freedom is the one way to test the possibilities of men, that under its stimulus men have risen from humblest origins to positions of dignity and trust, even though the fringes of freedom have also tempted others to lawlessness and the atrophy of civilized behavior. The basic query, in one form or another, remains forever before us.

The American impulse was for the experiment. Sensing this, Patrick Henry, with wonder in his voice, arose and said, "Gentlemen, we are in a state of nature."

iii. A New Kind of Man

OBSERVERS soon detected the presence of
a new kind of man in the New World
—a man variously seen as retrograded,
or as the dreamed-of "natural man," or as a symbol of a new
freedom and a new confidence in the future.

Dr. Benjamin Rush, writing to a friend in Europe in 1798, recognized the divergence from the old pattern.

The manner of settling a new country [he wrote] exhibits a view of
the human mind so foreign to the views of it which have been taken
for many centuries in Europe. [And again] This passion for migration . . . will appear strange to an European. To see men turn their
backs upon the houses in which they drew their first breath—upon the
church . . . upon the graves of their ancestors—upon their friends and
companions of their youth—and upon all the pleasures of cultivated
society, and exposing themselves to all the hardships and accidents of
subduing the earth, and thereby establishing settlements in the wilderness, must strike a philosopher on your side the water as a picture of
human nature that runs counter to the usual habits and principles of
action in man. But this passion, strange and new as it appears, is wisely
calculated for the extension of population in America.

Calculated, the good doctor means, by Providence, always to be counted on in the natural order of things. But, since his eye was on the practical advantages of settlement for the American future, the doctor went no further, to consider the psychological impact of this exodus upon the actors, or upon the future of science, art, and letters in America.

The theme of retrogression was certain to find voice. William Byrd's portrait of "Lubberland," the North Carolina boundary of around 1728, is too well known to need repetition here; and even Crèvecoeur's enthusiasm for the "new man," the American, is qualified by his characterization of the frontiersman as half savage. To both Crèvecoeur and Dr. Rush, the first wave of frontiersmen soon acquired traits of the semisavage, passing their lives in hunting and fishing, drinking excessively, living in dirt in wretched cabins, uneasy when civilization and its laws approached. The solitary life, said Crèvecoeur, renders the frontiersman "ferocious, gloomy and unsociable." "Above all," said Dr. Rush, "he revolts against the operation of the laws"; and hence he soon moves on and gives way to the second settler, the cultivator of the soil. Yet even this man, according to the doctor, works but half-heartedly, and "is seldom a good member of civil or religious society"; and, though "with high ideas of liberty," he spends overmuch time drinking and attending political meetings. It is the third settler, in the doctor's view, who becomes the man of character and solid property.[1] And Hugh Henry Brackenridge's *Modern Chivalry* is full of satire and humor on the follies of the Pennsylvania frontier.

Timothy Dwight, Federalist, however laudatory of his own Connecticut valley in his *Greenfield Hill,* has but to visit Vermont, a few miles to the north, settled in part by his own neighbors, to complain of the first wave of settlers as restless, shiftless, and lawless. "They are impatient of the restraints of law, religion and

[1] Benjamin Rush, *Essays, Literary, Moral and Philosophical,* 2d ed., pp. 213, 223.

morality," he writes. "At the same time," he adds caustically, "they
are usually possessed in their own view of uncommon wisdom."
The type, Dwight observes, "loves this irregular, adventurous, half-
working and half-lounging life; and hates the sober industry and
prudent economy by which his bush pasture might be changed into
a farm." Instead, selling out, moving on, he "becomes less and less
a civilized man." [2]

De Tocqueville extends Dwight's irony to Americans in general:
they "are not very much from believing themselves to be a distinct
species of mankind." Though the Frenchman gives less space to the
frontier than it perhaps warranted, he agrees that its inhabitants
"display, to a certain extent, the inexperience and rude habits of a
people in their infancy," meaning by "infancy" the lack of the
formal institutions of an older society. [3] Yet each of these observers,
in one form or another, represented a more privileged level of
society: Byrd as aristocrat, the two Frenchmen as visitors from a
hierarchical society, Rush as a prominent physician and writer, and
Dwight as Federalist, neo-Puritan, Anglophile, and imitator of the
Augustan Wits, lifting his nose at the odor of Jeffersonianism on
the breeze.

As the American moved westward his crudities and his bristling
independence of spirit did not diminish. Behind him rose the little
hamlets that so depressed Mrs. Frances Trollope. The favorite
phrase, "I'm as good as you are," she warned, "would soon take the
place of the law and the Gospel"; and she did not hesitate to lay
the blame at Jefferson's door, whose writings, she says, were "gen-
erally circulated" and "a mighty mass of mischief."

A little incident from Mrs. Trollope may test even now our
residue of frontier humor. To her it was a "brutal history," and a
"national degradation," words which few of us, one surmises, would
deem wholly appropriate. The Duke of Saxe-Weimar was travelling

---

[2] Timothy Dwight, *Travels in New-England and New-York* [*sic*], II, 440–441.
[3] Alexis de Tocqueville, *Democracy in America*, ed. Phillips Bradley, I, 334.

in this country in the 1830's, and had engaged for himself and suite seats in a stagecoach. An anonymous traveller who had likewise purchased a seat climbed in and made himself comfortable. The Duke, "in a very princely manner," a phrase open, we may assume, to varying interpretations, insisted that the man vacate his seat. Thereupon the driver "resolutely told the Duke that the traveller was as good, if not a better man than himself; and that no altera- tion . . . could be permitted." At this, the Duke threatened the driver with "the application of the bamboo." It was a mistake.

Down leaped our driver from his box, and peeling himself for the combat, he leaped about the vehicle in the most wild-boar style, calling upon the prince of a five acre patch to put his threat into execution. [The Duke then protested that he would complain to the governor.] This threat was almost as unlucky as the former, for it wrought the individual into a fury . . . and he swore that the Governor might go to——, and for his part he would just as lief lick the Governor as the Duke; he'd like no better fun than to give both Duke and Governor a dressing in the same breath; could do it, he had little doubt, etc., etc.; and instigating one fist . . . into the face of the marvelling and panic- stricken nobleman, with the other he thrust him down into a seat along- side the traveller . . . and bidding the attendants jump in . . . he mounted his box in triumph and went on his journey.[4]

Such were some of the external features of the new frontier, that era that lay between the wilderness of the original aborigines and the conventional little Main Streets that marked its end. From the beginning its men welcomed the opportunity to defy the old cate- gories, to ignore the ancient duties and enforced loyalties. For their hazards and their special skills they exacted the reward of exemption from the old assessments, impressments, confinements, and regula- tions. True, the frontier knew neither the cultural heritage of Europe nor the science of the Age of Enlightenment. It represented the loss of much, the negation of much. It was rarely religious or intellectual.

[4] Frances Trollope, *Domestic Manners of the Americans*, pp. 265–266.

It was, as observers noticed, a place where men accepted a semi-savage state and came to prefer it. And as the first frontier passed, it was replaced by settlements which had small glamor and which tended to repeat in simpler forms the old patterns of law and order, civil institutions, churches, and schools, with less of novelty than might have been expected from so independent a people.

And yet, while it lasted, that frontier was the source of the strongest of emotions, and it put its mark upon all America. It represented asylum from law, domesticity, bankruptcy, and poverty, from boredom, routine, and parental rigidity. It called to the adventuresome, the hardy, the rebellious, the less successful within established communities, the economically ambitious, the entrepreneur, the uprooted, the solitary seeker. Speculators exploited it hot upon the Revolution; and the east patronized it even while resenting the condescension of Europe, even while romanticizing the legend of its "natural man." Europe, said Emerson, reached to the Appalachians; beyond that was the west. Soon the Ohio, the Mississippi, the Missouri were the west; then Kansas, Texas, California; and last of all the Rocky Mountain fastnesses. The theme persisted, persists still in degenerated forms. Hamlin Garland, whose parents were of the second wave, said that his father's favorite remark was, "I'll never take the back trail," and his favorite ditty:

> Then over the hills in legions, boys;
> Fair freedom's star
> Points to the sunset regions, boys.

The raw west, of course, was not exactly what Jefferson had envisaged. Jefferson was an eighteenth-century mind, a Renaissance man on the edges of the colonial frontier, and his concept of nature was neither Puritan nor Romantic. Nature as untamed landscape full of ennobling messages was a later development. When Jefferson wrote of men as having the right to assume "the separate and equal station to which the Laws of Nature and Nature's God entitle them,"

or when Joel Barlow predicted that "as long as we follow nature in
politics as in morality, we are sure to be right," neither intended the
slightest concession to the Puritan connotation for nature, Winthrop's "liberty of corrupt nature," by which *sumus omnes deteriores*
(we are all worse) and which can be corrected only by submission
to authority. Nor, on the other hand, were they anticipating the
semisavage white on the farther frontiers. Instead they were employ-
ing the word *nature* in an eighteenth-century manner, with connotations of immutable laws by which the Creator in his benevolence
governed men and matter alike, laws uncovered and illustrated by
Newton's mathematics and Locke's psychology. They were thinking
neither of sunsets and waterfalls nor of uninhibited and bestial man.

Yet there was a connection. When Locke wrote, "In the beginning, all the world was America," he was referring to the semi-
fictional man who was antecedent to the original social compact.
Man in the natural state, before states had come into being, unhampered by tradition or restraints upon his natural liberty but experiencing the disadvantages of every man for himself, starting with
experience and reasoning upon his experience, had gradually found
the way to a communal polity which should at the same time offer
advantages to all and protection to each, within those inherent
rights antecedent to states. If this were true, where better might
natural rights and the natural man be studied in the living present
than in the untouched American forests, in the simple savage, and
in the free frontiersman, "the Adam before the naming," as it has
been put?

Again the shock of geography had tested old assumptions. If men
were originally free, and began social institutions from their original
social contracts—they did not have to be written—the new man in
America could be said to have reverted to that same freedom, not to
refuse all social living but to build anew from his own experience,
to frame his own institutions in the light of his own fresh experience
and his own best judgments. For governments and cultural patterns

were relative matters (Montesquieu had so taught) all but absent in the purer state, adopted by sensible men because rational and useful, but always subject to re-examination. Such a view was surely not far distant from the philosophy that animated the founding fathers in the liberties they took with their inheritance from the past.

On the more intellectual side, the answers of the New World arose in response to a present and a practical need, subject to the venerable past only insofar as the old might accommodate itself to the need. The reasoning behind the American Revolution reached the general public, no doubt in diluted form; but that it did touch even the frontier is shown by the presence of books, few in number but valued, even in the occasional log cabin, whose prototype furnished Lincoln with his clear if limited education in the principles of Jefferson.

It took time, of course, for the colonies to move toward the change. But as early as 1717, John Wise, son of an indentured servant and a graduate of Harvard, drawing generously on the German Baron Pufendorf, just issued in English in England, unites reason and feeling in the phrase "the dictates of Right Reason excited by the moving suggestions of humanity." [5] Thus the laws of nature, discoverable by clear reason, may be reinforced by direct experience, and feeling may serve not as an end but as provocation to reflection. Wise may quote a German Baron, but it is with the excitement of a son of toil who has discovered that he too may pit his strength against an arbitrary Andros or a Mather oligarchy, relying for his acts not on the traditional humbleness of petition but on the appeal to the common sense of man as man. Franklin, too, exhibits this same steady confidence in self with no undue qualms about humble origins, rising from simple beginnings to stand before parliaments and kings; and Jefferson, scholar though he was, was half frontiersman, and put into the Declaration of Independence a concept of

[5] John Wise, *Vindication of the Government of New England Churches,* p. 31.

government which sought no sanctions from monarchs or ecclesiastic power, a concept which he labelled the "common sentiments of the day." Perhaps it is no exaggeration, then, to suggest that the founding fathers, far as they were from romanticizing the frontier or from being themselves frontiersmen, nevertheless reflected something of that common experience.

William Carlos Williams, in an essay sprinkled with the insights of a poet, entitled "Against the Weather," recalls that Washington the frontiersman, when Braddock's disciplined redcoats ran into ambush and panic, *gave his men their liberty* and they, no doubt with silent whoops, took over and saved what could be saved.[6] Ruxton, mentioned below, tells the same thing of the raw American troops he saw in action in Mexico. Indifferent to uniforms, undisciplined, careless of appearance, rowdy, in action they suddenly became each man an independent unit functioning for the whole. This was the difference. Give men their individual liberties —or need we say "give," since each took it as his own right and saw no one empowered to give without the consent of the rest? —let each find his own tree or rock in disorderly, yet self-disciplined, response to the common need, and what might not yet be saved? This kind of result can never be achieved with slaves, for behind it lies the habit of self-direction. Once more the direct lessons of experience triumphed over manual and ritual designed for the predictable circumstance, and American confidence received a new impetus toward a native self-reliance.

America was, in a very real sense, the laboratory for a reconsideration of the common man and his potential for future good or evil, a notice to old dynasties and tyrannies that the evidence was not yet all in, and that unaccustomed liberties might elicit new answers. The shock of geography had been considerable. It had shaken static assumptions as to social layers. It had challenged the Puritan convic-

[6] William Carlos Williams, "Against the Weather," in *Selected Essays*, pp. 196–218. Read also "The American Background," pp. 134–161.

tion of the innate depravity of man as man. It had encouraged a
new hope for improvement in the human status under education,
information, and freedom, and had suggested that the common man
was indeed endowed with his share of common sense and reason,
that he might constitute a hitherto untested reservoir of good judgment and basic wisdom under trial. Reinforced by the new Age of
Reason, the new geography had foreseen a benign future as men's
minds comprehended the divine economy within the orderly laws
of progress. Where else than in this joint climate of geography and
opinion shall we find a source for America's incurable political
optimism in its fresher days? Even Alexander Hamilton, no friend
of the common man, could say of the revolutionary argument, "We
had no occasion to look into old, musty documents, but wrote from
our hearts." Where else shall we seek the stimulus for whatever is
most native in the contributions of Emerson and Thoreau, Whitman
and Lincoln?

So we arrive, though with reservations, at a concept of a new kind
of man in the New World. These reservations cluster about the
extremes on the ever-moving frontier, symbol at once of a laudable
self-reliance and a reversion to semisavagery. Though hamlets,
villages, farms, and cities, themselves duplicates of a soberer life,
pushed the frontier ever westward, that frontier continued to exert
its pull to hazard, lawlessness, and even a sordid brutality. Let us
face this aspect of the New Man in a separate chapter.

iv. Nature at Bay—The Cult of the Badman of the West[1]

IN OUR SEEMING CELEBRATION of the frontier theme in American life we have not overlooked the possibility that losses might outweigh gains. In the negative column we must surely admit a withering of the cultural inheritance, the heavy price in isolation and in loss of communal virtues. How intolerable indeed must have been the burden of existence in the older lands, or how heady the lure of adventure and new opportunity, when habit and home, castle and cathedral, pomp and circumstance encompassing authority, and above all the humbler ties binding human folk could no longer hold a man from loneliness and the risks of a savage frontier. Yet man cannot deny civilization, however poorly constituted, without raising the old Hobbesian ghost of its opposite, a life "solitary, poor, nasty, brutish and short." The man who lives to himself, said Aristotle, must needs be a beast or a god.

The frontier had its share of the beast in man. The most curious facet of that legacy, however, and one not provided for in Turner's

[1] This chapter is based on an article, slightly revised, by the author, "The Cult of the Bad Man of the West," *Texas Quarterly,* V (Autumn, 1962), 311–320.

thesis of the democratizing contribution of the west, is the persistent glorification of the one-time badman of the west. All nations must have their legendary heroes, figures whose deeds defy the careless years. Yet where but in the American west have those heroes been so recent, and where else has that hero been so completely the outlaw, the conscienceless killer, the open defier of law and order?

For there is in the far west, and no denying it, a definite cult of the badman, the callous, sullen, reckless master of the six-shooter, the cankered symbol of something summoned up as "the good old days." As a matter of actual record, he was the product of a very brief period, flourishing mainly in the interim between the original mountain man, scout, and explorer, and the sober settlements that signalized the end of the first frontier and the recovery of sanity. Nor would one pretend for a moment that the gunman, the bad character, *was* the west, or that he dominated it. Old-timers will tell you that if you kept out of his part of town, you might scarcely know of his existence; and were it not for this exaltation of his role, we might ignore him as we do the occasional saloon brawler. Why, then, has he become for no small segment of the population a symbol for that which is labelled heroic, and, more, the source of a welling satisfaction and jubilation when that "Old West" is publicly reconstructed?

There is no questioning the factual base of his existence. Too many contemporary accounts are available. Nor is the student of American history unaware that the frontier was always subject to lawlessness, reckless behavior, and deeds of violence. From the first misgivings of John Smith, or of William Bradford (of 1641–1642), through Crèvecoeur's comment, or Ruxton's report on the Americans in Santa Fe in 1848 as "the dirtiest, rowdiest crew I have ever seen collected together," the fact is recorded. Yet Ruxton somewhat modified his view upon closer acquaintance, though he continued to see the frontier mountain men as "white Indians," "hardy as bears," fierce, cruel to the point of sadism, insensitive to pain, resolute in peril, resourceful, a breed to command wonder and a begrudging respect.[2] But none of these earlier commentators had envisioned the coming bully of the cowtown and mining camp, the killer with a reputation for ruthless immediacy in murder. Mark Twain's *Roughing It* more reliably defined the type in Virginia City, Nevada, in the 1860's, "where a person is not respected until he has 'killed his man'."

It is legitimate enough, then, to inquire why this glorification of a vicious and brutal type. And who are the glorifiers of these ghouls of casual bloodshed? Some are the softer tourist breed, seeking titillation in the lonely spaces, though unlikely themselves to challenge even the lowly jackrabbit; some are young journalists who thrive on inflation of the melodramatic and the pseudoprodigious; still others are steady devourers of pulp fiction and haunters of the TV screen. But more are the rank and file of inhabitants of the great Rocky Mountain region, ready at the drop of the hat to take on by innocuous proxy all eastern belittlers of the land of peaks and mesas. A few, it might be added, are purveyors of "western" history and writers of some reputation. What unites them all is the quick response to any appeal to the "great old days of the badman of the west," though their concept of his reality be as ersatz as the Indian scalping party at the next local rodeo.

Let us be more specific. Here, for example, is a compilation of newspaper column sketches by one Boyce House, entitled *Cowtown Columnist*. Mr. House has written other books, all marked by a lively gusto when it comes to Texas legend, oil booms, cattleman days, and assorted wonders out of the Texas past. His readers expect from him readability, a swift narrative style, and a length not overextended, plus a mixture of Texas sentiment and native lore. "The Glory That Was" is the heading for one section of his compilation, and a gory collection of deeds it is, a glorification of the "great men" of a lawless era, culminating in El Paso and a burst of allitera-

[2] See Chapter V for comment on Ruxton.

tion, "the greatest galaxy of gunslingers ever gathered in a single spot." "Names that sound like bells," says James D. Horan in a contribution to Robert West Howard's *This is the West,* "they shone like angry comets above the mesas."

Texas was wild in its infancy, without a doubt. According to the same Mr. House, Land Commissioner Borden in 1835 reported that three hundred to four hundred land claims in a single county were probably spurious, and that in 1845 over 55 per cent of Texas land scrip was probably fraudulent. As late as 1886, House reports, an area twice the size of New York State was held by hardly 5,000 men, mostly in violation of such law as there was. Such statistics stir Mr. House to a rush of pride in his state, as do the deeds of violence, sometimes labelled "knighthood in Texas." It is but fair, however, to credit Mr. House with an impartial admiration for deeds of bravery (or recklessness) in the face of threat and against great odds, whether the doer be lawbreaker or law-enforcer. Such impartiality is likewise in the western tradition; for "a good man" may mean, primarily, good at what he undertakes. At any rate, House's is a Texas of perpetual action, frequent assaults upon the scenic calm, physical vitality, "guts," defiance, individualism, all amid a setting of drab frontier hamlets, saloons, boardwalks, and the treeless spaces that stretched in all directions.

Take John Wesley Hardin, "credited with having killed no less than forty men," himself killed by one Selman, in turn killed by a man who was also later killed. Or take Sam Bass, "beloved bandit," dead at twenty-seven after two brief years of train robberies. Two separate monuments to Bass have been whittled away by souvenir hunters, and a third stands awaiting further hero worship. Or take, as late as 1927, the Santa Claus robbery, a holiday feat by a robber-leader disguised as Saint Nicholas, which ended in six dead, three of them officers of the law, eight wounded, and an aftermath of mob lynching. Or consider Ben Thompson, "prince of pistoleers," who

began by killing Negro soldiers and police after the Civil War, killed
a sheriff who tried to disarm him, fled to New Orleans, where he
emerged alive from a duel with knives in a dark room, to kill another army officer, a few Mexicans, a saloonkeeper and a bartender,
and then was elected sheriff of Austin, the state capital of Texas.
During his tenure, it is said, Austin was free from killings. After a
further killing in San Antonio, Thompson was hauled in triumph
through the streets of Austin; but his day was about over, and he
sank into gambling, drinking, and wild escapades until shot down in
San Antonio. "Greatest of the Southwest's bad men," exults Mr.
House.

Nor can we omit Billy the Kid, whose final resting place is likewise a Mecca for tourists, a development which mere propinquity
will not explain, for the hamlet of Lincoln, New Mexico, is remote,
and the same tourists might refuse to pause, even for a brief tribute,
at Hannibal, Missouri, or Concord, Massachusetts. Lincoln, New
Mexico, a guide book (not Mr. House's) assures us, boasts "more
than twenty-five markers within two city blocks" to the deeds of
this bad boy, whose tombstone, like Bass's, to quote the same authority, "the souvenir chippers got." What other figure in human
history has been commemorated with markers for twenty-five separate manifestations within the space of two blocks?

Billy was, like John Wesley Hardin, but twenty-seven when
he died—"heroic" Billy, who told a former companion stricken with
a broken thigh, to lie still so that Billy would not disfigure his face
when he put a bullet through his head. Yet sadism was not limited
to the outlaw; for House's "The Last Man that Billy the Kid Killed"
relates the repeated tauntings of Billy's jailer, his reminders of the
hammers busy at erecting a scaffold for Billy, and his repeated loving
pats on his holster, saying meanwhile, "Why don't you make a break,
so I can have the pleasure of shooting you down?" Billy outwitted
him, too, giving him just time to stare into cold blue eyes above the

barrel of a gun before he became number twenty-one, "not counting Indians and Mexicans." Kindly, moronic Billy and "The Glory That Was."

Or there comes to hand a popular handbook of the west, entitled *It's an Old Wild West Custom,* whose author, Duncan Emerich, was, at the time of its writing, chief of the Folklore Section of the Library of Congress. Herein the west is lauded as vast, variegated, and unconquered, the setting for roughness, toughness, and tall tales. Again we encounter the same gusto over the badman, especially in a chapter entitled "To Die With Boots On," envisioned as a glamorous and ennobling end.

Or take a more ambitious text, *A Treasury of Western Folklore,* compiled by Benjamin A. Botkin, a folklore specialist. Here the narrator ranges widely by means of a considerable selection of readings loosely held together under sundry groupings. In this book the gunman is crowned as America's "most heroic symbol, next to the cowboy." Let us pause to contemplate but one of these heroic figures, one Clay Allison, who drifted to Texas and New Mexico after the Civil War, but not before he had killed a neighbor in a macabre duel with knives in an open grave. Allison ran into a gunman in the west who aspired to round out his killings to fifteen—because he liked to see them fall. He and Allison, carousing together, agreed upon a duel on horseback, firing until one was dead—but not until they had eaten together. At the hotel table, surrounded by others attracted by the novel situation, Allison suddenly drilled his opponent between the eyes and, as the man fell face forward onto his plate, calmly continued to eat, bidding the others do likewise. Then he announced that, because of an indisposition on the part of his opponent, the duel was called off. Allison later managed to kill a sheriff, but met his own end when a heavy wagon wheel passed over his drunken head. Botkin couples Allison with Billy the Kid for the hall of fame.

Mr. Bernard De Voto, Utahan in origin, set the tone for this

Botkin volume by a defiant Preface, written with overt contempt for the pallid easterner and a kind of truculent pride in the contemplation of the raw west, violent, unreliable, dwarfing man's pretensions, accepting to its company only those who can stand up to it. The slap at the easterner seems gratuitous, since most westerners are but easterners once or twice removed. A westerner is best defined simply as a man who has come to terms with the west, whatever his birthplace; many of the best came directly from the long-worked farms of Europe. Besides, since the old west lingers today in fragmented forms only, De Voto's blast would seem somewhat belatedly inspired.

Nevertheless, Mr. De Voto gives us a key to our puzzle. The old west was a tough land, and it did make excessive demands on individuals. The names upon the land still echo the facts: Bad Water, Bad Lands, Dry Springs, No Wood, Starved Butte, Freezeout Mountains, Rattlesnake Flats, Alkali Flats, Lost Corral, Lost Cabin, Lone Tree, Poison Spider, Cactus Flats, Burial Rock, Tombstone. It was no place for the weakling, and it gave no quarter to those who gave up. We are talking now not of badmen, but of all who came. The mildest of men set afoot or on horseback among these spaces quickly shed his amiability and adopted fortitude and resolution as his lot. The biggest braggart came soon to the center of his boasting, accepting the common measure of testing: "Can he really take it?" Swift decision, action in peril, endurance in the monotony of time and space and ever-present danger became the expectation of all. If it was not Indian, it was grizzly bear, or drouth, or sandstorm, or prairie fire, or waterless plains and treeless horizons, or blizzard, or plain misery and starvation. And if the Indian came circling and yelping, every man, woman, and child moved swiftly into the ring of wagons and tried to make each shot true and without waste. There was no time for book morality or metaphysical debate. All codes underwent the same swift simplification and a man soon tested the resources of his central being.

Small wonder if for those inured to these experiences, the same swift "justice" carried over to whites who betrayed, robbed, or threatened violence without due cause. In the tight circle banded against imminent death, the desperado might be the most valuable of men, and competition arose for such reputations, whatever the setting; nor did the easy transfer from Indian fighter to frontier marshall or frontier badman mean much in the way of special prestige. As those of us in the ranks of World War I remember, under stress the lines were not sharp between educated and uneducated, criminal and law-abiding; nor did the officer caste half suspect the amount of frontline folklore on the sudden disappearance of those who relied overmuch on "authority." Not the accident of rank or status, but testing under strain proved the man.

The exigencies of the frontier spared no man because of previous servitude or previous fame. Think of the respectable businessmen en route to Denver in 1868, found staked to the plains with Indian fires built upon their abdomens, consuming their vitals. Think of the man who crawled for survival in a blizzard into the gutted carcass of a cow on the plains, only to find in the morning that he was frozen in, and mightily put to it to hack his way out with a single small blade. Think of the ordeal of Hugh Glass, as John Neihardt, with an eye to the Homeric, has recorded it.

But that first raw west changed. The Indians retreated to reservations, railroads cut thin lines of communication across the wastes, small towns sprang up, and ranches, outlying farms, cattle, mining camps. Then came the era of the badman, following on the original vanguard. Who was he? Botkin admits that the west "attracted, fostered and harbored the lawless, the reckless, the nomadic and the predatory, the unfit and the unadjusted." Why should such men add up to spell Botkin's "heroic"? Perhaps because there was in them the residue of man pitting his small self against the impossible, the dominant note still of resolution in the face of overwhelming odds. Insofar as the "hero" is the individual who stands out by deeds not

easily emulated by the "average," rising with more than ordinary
energies and indifference to risk life itself against hopeless odds, the
killer qualified often as hero. But if we demand the further in-
gredient of selflessness, as shown by consideration for the weak and
the defenseless before self or by self-sacrifice for friend, clan, or
country, then the badman fails woefully and is little more than the
lone gambler whose motives are not above suspicion; nor will the
occasional pretense of a Robin Hood motive serve to justify him.
This is a distinction which the West, in its ardor for swift action
and hardihood before danger, is apt to overlook; and it is why Lewis
and Clark, Jedediah Smith, or Father de Smet remain more truly
heroic.

Does it become clearer, then, that the badman was, or is, but one
element in the composite image which the West likes to build of
itself—the image of a taciturn toughness in response to a hard lot,
the solitude, the thankless labor, and the actually humble status of
the average man on his own in a new land? Above all, it is the image
and the code of resistance—resistance to weather and space and man's
absorption into impersonal institutions, to his exploitation by land
jobbers, land sharks, land laws, large landowners, mining com-
panies, and to the whole complicated encroachment once more of
civilization, with its multiplicity of denials of the individual's right
to be simply man. Quite apart from the gunman (who was, after all,
the exception), the average man who had come west in those earlier
days, denying himself all past ease to try himself against the raw
hazards of the untried, the man who spent months and years mostly
apart from society on the lonely plains or on the remote mining
claim, came to value himself as a man, not as a representative of
someone or something larger. And when he drifted occasionally to
some drab hamlet on the fringes of society, he composed his tanned
visage into denial of hardship and indifference to others, making for
the nearest bar, wary of what he inwardly thirsted for, companion-
ship. Such a pose, finally no longer pose but a kind of personality,

meeting with the same kind of response, could easily slide into truculence, a bottled-up resentment of defeat, a readiness to take quick offense. On every face he read the same message: "Don't tread on me. No one pushes me around; I don't need you. I can take care of myself." In a land of individuals whose code, however rough, was that of noninterference in a quarrel, a man had a chance to be recognized as such.

We need not deny, of course, the other side of the shield, the open-handed hospitality of the isolated ranch or cabin, the genuine hand of welcome to the stranger—America, says D. W. Brogan, is the only land where "Howdy, stranger," is not a threat. But we are seeking the motivation of the less fortunate man, the rejected one, the un-successful, the itinerant cowboy, the nomad of hard labor, who in his most desperate stage of badman still symbolized man in resist-ance, man endeavoring to assert himself against anonymity.

For this simpler story, we might turn to a reminiscence issued in 1942 by the Texas Folklore Society, the memoirs of an American of the older Scotch-English stock whose life had been that of a common laborer, cowboy, tie-cutter, in the out-of-doors, with intervals of escape into the relief of hunting and fishing ("the only way to have a genuinely good time," he wrote of three and a half months of total solitude on the Neches River). Here was a man with no malice in him, a wandering bachelor, fond of children but rarely seeing them, seeking too late a lost Eden, knowing quite well that that day was gone.

Yet Solomon Wright had a code, too, one almost identical with that of the older west, minus the touch of violence. Listen: "Attend strictly to your own business, and treat everybody strictly right in every respect, and give everybody to strictly understand that they must treat you in the same way; ask no favors of anybody, and grant none only to those you know will appreciate them. Above all things, don't allow yourself to be flattered." This is the authentic note of self-respect, independence, mistrust of society in the large, preference

for the self-chosen path, taciturnity, wariness of self-delusion—all
on the humblest of social levels. This it is to be American when one
is not one of the privileged. But inject into such a man a dash of
resentment, a bad temper, and a conviction that society's hand is
raised against him, and you have one who could be pushed to lawlessness, even if initially by accident or uncalculated impulse to resist
injustice. "Resist, resist," said Walt Whitman; but he did not mean
to the point of the badman's code; he meant resist all that belittles
a man as man.

But let us glance at a more recent example of violence, this time
from northwestern Wyoming, as recorded in the newspapers of
Wyoming around March and April of 1939. Earl Durand was a
sturdy lad of ranch background, born around 1913, patterning himself as boy on the Daniel Boone legend, becoming in time a fine shot,
a skilled hunter, an indefatigable walker, capable of covering forty
miles in a day—in short, in our urban terms, a withdrawn character.
In 1939, at twenty-six, he was a lone wolf, six-feet-two, bearded, 250
pounds of muscle and sinew, acquainted with the deeper wilds of the
Absaroka range, indifferent to people.

Like Natty Bumppo, Durand was destined to come into conflict
with the game laws, nothing uncommon in mountain areas; but,
unlike Natty, he had nowhere to retreat. He was arrested and housed
in the Cody, Wyoming, jail for killing a bull elk. It was not difficult
for him to break out, taking a deputy with him as hostage. Had he
paused here and returned to accept his sentence, he might still have
made an adjustment in a sparsely settled country. But he chose to
take on society singlehanded. Pursued, he shot two deputies with
three shots, and then hid out in a steep-walled canyon in the mountains. Knowing now his general whereabouts, society rallied for the
chase, importing bloodhounds from Colorado, gas bombs, and
eventually a Montana National Guard detachment, complete with
howitzer and soker mortar. A three-day battle followed. Two posse-
men attempted a run, but Durand picked them off with one shot

each. He had killed four men. There was now no retreat for him. When the posse finally reached the hideout and the dead men, Durand was gone.

Shortly after, at two in the afternoon, he entered a Powell bank and lined up the nine employees against a wall. Why he attempted this foolhardy invasion of a small city is unknown; perhaps he wished to go out in the grand style. At any rate, Powell was soon alive with guns, rifles, and pistols. Citizens responded in kind, more in excitement than in hatred; Durand had thrown down the gauntlet, and the "good old days" were back once more. Using three employees, tied with shoelaces, as a shield, Durand attempted to leave the building. He was met with a hail of bullets of all descriptions, which shattered all the bank's windows and peppered the walls, but managed only to kill one of the employees. Then a seventeen-year-old boy, taking careful aim with a 30-30, hit Durand in the chest. Durand crawled back into the bank and shot himself in the head. Perhaps the story throws some light on the dramas of the past. In another day, what a frontier marshall Durand would have made!

For how recent the old west is. There are still old people who remember that era and how it was. As late as 1930, Frank Linderman wrote in *American* the tale of an Indian then still living on the Crow Reservation who had never seen a white man until he participated at twenty-five in the destruction of Custer's band. He had been born where Sheridan, Wyoming, now stands. As recently as 1880, Wyoming territory had but 14,000 men and 5,000 women and children. Even in 1928 a census of some seven hundred of the students at Wyoming's state university showed less than half born in the state, hardly 6 per cent of their parents, and but one in a thousand of their grandparents.[3]

Not surprisingly, then, echoes of the past linger in the lore of the

[3] W. O. Clough, "Wyoming and the Westward Movement," *American Journal of Sociology*, XXXV (1930), 808–815.

gaudier deeds that enlivened an otherwise uneventful routine. The badman, as we can see now, was the end of an experiment, the blind alley of one side of the frontier, the last word in freedom from responsibility. It is curious to reflect, however, that his dates almost exactly paralleled those of the great robber barons of the East, likewise a predatory, ruthless set of individuals denying the claims of a social responsibility. It is customary to treat these gentlemen of great wealth as products of a "social Darwinism," an economic interpretation of the doctrine of survival of the fittest. It is more likely that they arose in a postwar North as a kind of final testing of a frontier laissez-faire psychology, even as the badman came often from a postwar South to test in defeat and resentment the cul-de-sac of a frontier individualism. Survival of the fittest was merely a convenient and contemporary term to palliate a ruthless disregard of the general welfare in either case. Again we confront the old dichotomy of Hobbes versus Locke, Hobbes always reminding us that brutish competition remains within society, Locke more optimistically asserting that reason, too, leavens society, else society would long since have perished.

The classic example of the badman's end was in Virginia City, Montana (not to be confused with Mark Twain's Virginia City, Nevada); and the classic account appears in Thomas J. Dimsdale's little book *Vigilantes of Montana,* long rare, but happily reissued in 1953. This mining town in a mountain valley, now a well-planned tourist museum spot, was the scene of more than one hundred killings in brawls, robberies, holdups, and calculated murders. Respected citizens on their way home with provisions might be found dead in the willows, their horses stolen and their family provisions scattered. No one was safe. The road gangs, so-called, laughed at terror, ridiculed opposition, and openly threatened retaliation on any who protested. Far from being the "glory that was," the situation was more nearly analogous to that of today's adolescent bullies whose excuse for killing, when a citizen hesitates to yield money, car, or wife, is, "He asked for it, didn't he?" For the true bully knows no law but that of a demented ego.

There was but one possible solution. An aroused citizenry, acting swiftly and sworn to secrecy, elected officials and swore in deputies, who rounded up the villains, including the sheriff, Plummer, a leader in the depredations, and hanged twenty-two, after due trial before an armed jury. Often these deputies, alone or in two's, proceeded at great risk to lonely mountain cabins to demand surrender. The reign of terror ceased abruptly, and casual murder was no longer safe as a pastime in Virginia City, although just over the mountains in Idaho, in the succeeding months, some sixty killings took place in one community alone.

Dimsdale, editor of the paper, a young Englishman who had come west for his health, was concerned over the accusation in eastern papers that the vigilante action had been illegal. He insisted not only that the trials had been conducted with fairness and dignity and prisoners discharged against whom proof was not available, but especially that such vigilante action was consistent with the very origins of law within human society. Referring to an old Anglo-Saxon tradition, he viewed law not as permissive power handed down by distant authority, but as action arising from the very demand of a community proceeding in the name of mutual safety for themselves and their families. Montana, he pointed out, had no territorial judiciary, no official courts and officers or legal machinery; and the vigilantes had voluntarily disbanded upon knowledge that a territorial judge had finally been appointed from Washington. Thus spoke an ancient line of reasoning, one that lay behind the American Revolution and its justification, but one apparently better understood by a young Englishman than by scores of American citizens, then or today.

Dimsdale had no flattery for the average citizen. Too many of them cowered in acceptance of the situation, or connived at villainy by winking at flagrant violations of common decency, hoping thereby to be spared. Yet when the first condemned man's body was swaying above them, they pumped it full of a hundred bullets, and burned it afterward, with appropriate rowdiness. Law and order, Dimsdale reflected, came usually with the resolute action of a determined minority, no longer able to tolerate its opposite.

Such a tale puts both the badman and his admirer in a truer perspective. As a lone individual, going down to inevitable defeat before encroachments on his right to be an individual, the badman might be made to symbolize something like a solitary will pitted against tragic odds and still refusing to surrender. But as a mob, a gang, even as a way for each single man in society, he became an impossible standard to follow, a threat to the body civil. His admirer, then, had also to give way to the demands of the larger society, even if that too had its own forms of injustice. This is the eternal structure of human living with its dual necessities, the rights of the individual and the rights of the communal group.

To the always individualistic frontier, the reckless killer might seem to have thrown down the gauntlet, however vainly, before the ever-swelling tide of tradition and a tasteless conformity, and to be the last defender of the man without a voice before the courts of established privilege. Many a Hollywood western still revolves about the simplified theme of the little man in conflict with the big banker, the big landholder, and a corrupt constabulary hand in hand with injustice; and the front rows still resound with cheers as the silk-hatted and cravatted representatives of privilege reach final justice. The hero, the good sheriff, is also pitted on many an occasion against these same corrupt defenders of the status quo. Rebellion against railroads, the hired enforcers of "economic progress," the intimidations of a complicated law, all the harassments and complexities of an entrenched civilization made for the privileged, seemed to the wild man of the west, as to the Indian, and even to some settlers, the only gesture left before his manhood went down to a final defeat.

Yet the badman was no less doomed, in the long run, than the last bison and the last Indian rally against the rush for land and gold.

The badman may have been originally simply a bad man, or an escapee from earlier crime, or a prematurely hardened youth running away from early mistreatment (there were many such); or he may have been a badly scared man, lonely and baffled, confronted by a faceless landscape and the rawness of an unsettled land, a man who had made his boast, proved his defiance, and so got into depths from which there was no retreat. Here Stephen Crane's masterly story, "The Blue Hotel," written in the mid-nineties, proves its understanding; for the Swede was just such a novice from the east, dreading the testing of his courage, rising to the test as he conceived it to be (after all, Johnnie did cheat, and the code demanded calling his bluff); and then, overconfident when he thought his initiation accomplished, he met his death after all, even as he had feared.

The badman's lawlessness, therefore, does not signify that he alone knew resentment and frustration. Resentments we have always with us, as the Populist movement of the 1890's proved. How to retrieve the losses, how to force the readjustment of an unfair balance, how to sublimate the resentments, legitimate or fancied, these are the permanent problems, individually or socially. The shallow adulation of the killer by the unthinking is hardly to be recommended as a social phenomenon; yet in the last analysis, it may not be the callous killings, the sadism, the brutality, that attracts, but something deep in the heart of man, the strange and desperate dream of never to submit, never to be conquered, the force that compelled Milton to make a hero of his Satan, and made Melville cast his Captain Ahab in a heroic role.

The unselective tourist will not lead us far into the mystery. He is a tamed creature and will never draw his gun upon the invaders of his daily freedom, the ugly concession traps, the grotesque billboards, the mean-spirited leeches upon his family's small provision for travel. He is housebroken; and he knows that jobs are not always easy to find. His passing salute to the badman and his legend, half-jocular, half-historical, though not deep, may be still an atavistic stirring, whatever the price, of an old dream of freedom for every man. We always appeal to that dream in the masses when the nation is threatened; we do not so often stir it in the individual, for that is to court the unexpected. Yet that dream began in defiance of the accumulated burden of "Down, dog, down," and it rings in trumpet tones from the legend engraved about the base of Thomas Jefferson's statue in Washington—what man had the nerve to put it there?—"I have sworn on the altar of God eternal hostility against every form of tyranny over the mind of man." The badman had no mind to boast of, no political philosophy behind his deeds, only an insanity of rebellion; even so, the cult of the badman symbolizes in some crude and distorted way the endless hunger of the human animal for freedom in an inattentive world.

v. Whence a Native Literature?

WE HAVE LAID the foundation of wonder and change in a New World and the risks of the far frontier. We have not asked how these initial factors might affect the hope of a native literature. If the preceding chapters appear somewhat extreme in statement, the correctives are sufficiently available. Nevertheless, it is unlikely that any will deny the problem confronting the youthful nation in its ambition to achieve, among other things, a native literature. The gospel of America's promise was widely announced; and immigrants flocked to the shores of opportunity. Yet the emphasis was increasingly on the overt symbols of prosperity and energy and boistrous expansion. Emerson was far from the first to plead for "something better than the exertions of mechanical skill" to fulfill "the postponed expectation of the world." Bryant, in his earlier paper on American poetry in the *North American Review* of July, 1818, protested "the sickly and affected imitation" of English poets of his time (he himself was but twenty-four at the writing) and called for a greater encouragement of the native writer.

The early Republic was assailed by doubt and concern over the failure of the new freedoms to produce other than mechanical and economic results. Early magazines abounded in pleas for a native, a spontaneous literature, one clearly freed from the European past yet equalling it in prestige.[1] The uneasy feeling persisted that European snobbery toward America's lagging arts had a case. Jefferson had earlier begged Europe to be patient: "When we shall have existed as a people as long as the Greeks did before they produced a Homer, the Romans a Virgil, the French a Racine and Voltaire, the English a Shakespeare and Milton, should this reproach be still true, we will inquire from what unfriendly causes it has proceeded." [2]

Nevertheless the query persisted. What accounted for the delay? Where were the Americans to find the native materials? Who were to be the voices of the new Republic? What should be their themes, their models? One thing alone all agreed on: the new literature must not be imitative merely of the European past. Fears were even expressed that the floodtide of new immigrants who had not known the Revolution or shared in the common experience, or that the persistent reading of books from a feudal and undemocratic Europe, might delay or corrupt the native note. Charles Brockden Brown, one of America's first novelists, pictured in *Clara Howard* (1801) a young country lad corrupted by reading European books, for lack of a suitable democratic library, and so falling into a regretable reverence for royalty and a foreign contempt for an American "peasantry," a word not employed in the new land. Young ladies were felt to be peculiarly susceptible to such foreign, undemocratic influences, and early novels often warned them against the wiles of indiscriminate novel-reading and the seductions of red-jacketed British officers.

Two themes, however, seemed to be available to the aspiring American writer: the magnificent landscapes of the new world, still

---

[1] The topic of early magazines is well treated in various places, for example, Benjamin T. Spencer, *The Quest for Nationality;* also Perry Miller, *The Raven and the Whale.*

[2] Thomas Jefferson, *Notes on the State of Virginia,* ed. W. M. Peden, p. 64.

largely a wilderness, and the natural nobleman of the frontier and the soil. Under the first stimulus of the term "republic," there were those, too, who advocated a return to the simplicities of the ancient Greek and Roman republics. But this impulse was already dated, a remnant of the dignity attached to the signers of the Declaration and the first "fathers"; and the chief result, as an eighteenth-century gentry gave way to the rising sons of industry, was a rash of pseudo-classical architecture and a host of post-Revolution hamlets from New York State to Georgia, each located on the first wave of westward movement after the Revolution, named Troy, and Athens, Rome, Atlanta, Utica, and Syracuse.

Charles Brockden Brown attempted in some measure to recognize the new themes. In his Preface to *Edgar Huntley* he asserted, ". . . that the field of investigation, opened to us by our own country, should differ essentially from those which exist in Europe, may be readily conceived"; and he openly advocated the abandonment of "puerile superstitions and exploded manners, Gothic castles and chimeras" in favor of native materials. "The incidents of Indian hostility, and the perils of the Western wilderness," he wrote, "are far more suitable; and for a native of America to overlook these would admit of no apology." [3]

Unfortunately, enthusiasm over landscape and wildness was not sufficient for a literature of any depth; nevertheless, a thousand amateur ditties and descriptive passages took up the theme of our vast spaces, our majestic mountains, our great rivers, our Niagara Falls, our rocks and rills, and the "lessons" to be gained from them. They but proved once more that the versifying urge is no guarantee of talent.

The faults of these "female poetesses" of the 1830's are only too glaring: realism abandoned for romantic diffuseness; natural scenery enlisted as a handmaiden to hymnology, private quiverings confused

[3] Charles Brockden Brown, Preface, "To the Public," pp. iii–iv, in *Edgar Huntley*.

with cosmic awfulness, tremulous excursions along the banks of some "humble rill" used to reaffirm household virtues, vague aspirations heaving heavenward while safely anchored in loyalty to parish and kitchen; and all concluding with "O, may this to me a lesson be!"

One has but to consult Mr. Rufus W. Griswold's *The Female Poets of America* [4] to view the consequences. Here Mrs. Sarah Hale —and one or two examples will suffice—composes a poem to the Mississippi River, destined somehow to "usher in the reign of peace and love," while her own nearer "humble rill" is to roll through Time as her soul's tribute of "fervent gratitude" and "holy praise," not to the river but to the God who put the river there for Mrs. Hale's private edification so that she might conclude the whole chorus with admiration for the charms of "household love." The actual Mississippi is nowhere present.

And Miss Caroline May effuses thus "To Nature":

> Rocks, and woods, and water,
>   I am now with ye!
> What a grateful daughter
>   Ought I not to be!
> Alone with Nature—oh, what bliss,
>   What a privilege is this!

Her final stanza concludes:

> Loving ye, e'en when ye are
> From my loving heart afar.

The commas around rocks, and woods, and water, indicate the breathless and apparently mutual recognition of each separate phenomenon; the exclamation points indicate the whole ecstatic, earnest moment; and the final words pour upon nature the comfort of being

---

[4] Rufus W. Griswold, *The Female Poets of America*. See Mrs. Sarah Hale, "The Mississippi," p. 59, and Caroline May, "To Nature," p. 348.

loved by Miss Caroline May. The fact that *ye* appears both as nomi-native and accusative is obviously something that only a callous pedant would note. One begins to understand better the respect with which William Cullen Bryant's restraint was received.

For Bryant, almost alone of the earliest poets, maintained the dig-nity of his New England inheritance and the sincerity of a personal attachment to his boyhood surroundings. Freneau, it is true, had shown the way to some pre-Romantic use of native themes and land-scapes. But one has only to visit Cummington in western Massachu-setts, and the ancestral farm, set high up on the hills bordering the Westfield River, a branch of the Connecticut River, to put Bryant in perspective. The original smaller house still there, the remnants of the once enveloping forest, the little stream that still trickles down from the wooded hills, the absence of near neighbors, the lofty re-moteness from the little village in the valley, the silence that enwraps one on a summer day—all these enter vividly into Bryant's modest verses. Add to this natural setting the death there of mother and brother from tuberculosis, the labor in the fields with the stern, hard-driving Calvinist grandfather, the liberal Federalism of the doctor-father, and the common theme of nature and solitude in Bryant is not far to seek. Like Jonathan Edwards, whose home was not vastly different, the boy Bryant experienced many a silent walk in the forest shades, many a solitary hour of labor on the upland fields. In an agricultural age, such lonely farm backgrounds were a common heritage—Daniel Webster orating to the cornfields, Hawthorne skat-ing alone in the Maine woods, Thoreau surveying his neighbors' fields, Cooper growing up on his father's settlement project. No one knows now, said an old man in Orange County, New York, in the last days of the eighteenth century, how dark and gloomy these woods and swamps were before they were cleared off by man.

Bryant's "A Winter Piece," for example, written when he was but twenty-six, is as truly Cummington as Whittier's "Snow-Bound" is the Haverhill farm.

> The time has been that these wild solitudes,
> Yet beautiful as wild, were trod by me
> Oftener than now.

The landscape is that "in nature's loneliness," further touched by winter:

> When shrieked
> The bleak November winds, and smote the woods,
> And the brown fields were herbless . . .
> I sought, I loved them still; they seemed
> Like old companions in adversity.

Of course the note is Wordsworthian, as "Thanatopsis" echoes the British graveyard poets; but each is also drawn from Bryant's own meditation and lonely youth. So in "The Forest Hymn" the groves that "were God's first temples," the archetype for columns and pillars and arching branches, are divorced from human institutions and teach the elementary lesson of life and death and life renewed. "Let me often to these solitudes retire," concludes the poet; and, echoing an eighteenth-century rationalism:

> Be it ours to meditate
> In these calm shades, thy milder majesty,
> And to the beautiful order of thy works,
> Learn to conform the order of our lives.[5]

Whittier's later vision was likewise homebound. In each of these sober poets the ideal is clear: the simplicity of liberty in a rural setting. Whittier in "Among the Hills" makes it plainer—the man independent, sober, industrious, with his own few books, himself his own lawgiver, a man "equal to his home":

> A man to match his mountains, not to creep
> Dwarfed and abased below them.[6]

[5] Bryant, "A Winter Piece," p. 63; "A Forest Hymn," p. 75; and "The Prairies," p. 81, all in Harry H. Clark, *Major American Poets*.
[6] Whittier, "Among the Hills," *ibid.*, p. 165.

Whittier, too, was indebted to Wordsworth and to Burns; but neither of these Americans is Wordsworth. The English poet's sheep-herders and leechgatherers seem a docile lot, set in an inherited pattern, and virtuous insofar as they are humbly content within their lot, exuding lessons more to the poet than to themselves. Whittier's homesteader is his own lawgiver, inheritor of New England and Quaker independency; and Bryant's liberal conservatism as editor is well known.

Bryant visited the western prairies of Illinois once, in 1833, and attempted a poem of their impact upon him. "These fair solitudes," he repeats, where he dreams in the silent spaciousness of races now long forgotten and races to come:

> And my heart swells, while the dilated sight
> Takes in the encircling vastness . . .
> As if the ocean, in his gentlest swell,
> Stood still.

But Bryant's note was not that of westward expansion, and he re-mained the dignified, on occasion somewhat austere poet, never quite recapturing the purer organ note of "Thanatopsis," but maintaining the respect of his countrymen for his native theme. Washington Irving, one of the first to be born within the new federation, likewise failed to comprehend the new day. Like his own Rip Van Winkle, he dozed in the romantic past, the European-colonial phase of America, waking after his long absence in the Alhambra and West-minster Abby settings abroad to make a belated effort to bring him-self up to date. His excursion down the Ohio, down the Mississippi, and up the Arkansas River to the borders of modern Oklahoma was a praiseworthy attempt to understand, but it remains the work of a romantic; nor did his amanuensis labors for Astor or Captain Bonneville amount to a great deal more than a good job of public relations, an arousing of interest in the still-new west.

The other theme, that of the nobleman of nature, took its start perhaps with the figure of Daniel Boone, whose story, as related by John Filson in 1784, set the pattern even before Crèvecoeur and Benjamin Rush. And here we must pause a moment to note once more the strange pull of nature untamed. The evidence is before us; and more than one unlettered narrator admits on interview to this experience of an inner happiness, even amid hardship and lurking savages, a happiness not to be traded for all the lures of civilization, and having no source whatsoever in the artificial "noble savage" of European romanticism. For its roots are in personal experience and in a knowledge too deep for mere words. Occasionally it gets into literature, as we shall see; but it is not a major note there, in its simpler forms, perhaps because literature is a product of pen and paper rather than of the active life of the untutored.

Boone went early to Kentucky, "lately an howling wilderness, the habitation of savages and wild beasts . . . rising from obscurity to shine with splendor." In 1775 he returned to North Carolina to lead his family to the new land, "which I esteemed a second paradise." His women, he claimed, were the first white women ever to stand on the banks of the Kentucky River. His daughter was captured in 1776 by Indians, along with two other girls. Boone, with eight men, immediately pursued the Indians and recaptured the girls. Later captured himself and taken to the general area of Detroit, he made his escape after four months of captivity, and travelled alone for 160 miles in five days with but one meal. He lost two sons and a brother to the Indians, and much property, and spent, as he put it, "many dark and sleepless nights . . . a companion for owls." And yet Filson quotes Boone as saying, "I was happy in the midst of dangers and inconveniences. In such a diversity it was impossible I should be disposed to melancholy. No populous city, with all the varieties of commerce and stately structures, could afford so much pleasure to my mind, as the beauties of nature I found here." [7] Boone

[7] Quotations from Boone are from John Filson, *The Discovery, Settlement, and Present State of Kentucke*, pp. 49–50, 56, *et passim*.

notoriously evaded company, even that of later colonists, becoming a stranger even to his former neighbors, abandoning the past, seeking solitude.

It may be argued, of course, that Filson's portrait is embellished for popular consumption. Yet we have other more direct statements. One recalls, for example, Charles Goodnight, Texas cowman of a century later, reminiscing in his old age on the vast deserts and plains, outlaws, Mexican and Indian marauders, drought and heat, all of which, he said, "called on all a man had of endurance and bravery." Nevertheless, he added, "The happiest I have lived . . . Most of the time we were solitary adventurers in a great land as fresh and new as the spring morning, and we were free and full of the zest of darers." [8] The parallels might be multiplied—Jedediah Smith, pursuing to his death the next unmapped horizon, the frail Parkman, the elderly women of a still-remembered day who looked back with a quiet pride upon their share in the hardships of first settlement, expressing no regrets, only a kind of solid joy in the recollection.

The frontier had, it is true, its obverse of terror and fright, its deadening solitudes and the hazards of sudden attack. Women, in particular, must have trailed along with these reckless men in shrinking apprehension. Per Hansa's wife in Rölvaag's *Giants in the Earth* is unquestionably a realistic portrait of loneliness pushed to insanity; and the woman's role in the saga of the westward movement has probably never been adequately recognized.

But let us consider one further example of the secret happiness to be experienced in the solitudes of a new land, this time no American, but a young Englishman of cultivated antecedents, an officer in the British army, and one of the rare ones able to capture in writing something of the true experience.

George Frederick Ruxton had pushed his way in 1848, mostly alone, from Mexico City to New Mexico and southern Colorado,

[8] J. Evetts Haley, *Charles Goodnight, Cowman and Plainsman*, p. 259.

and there, where Pueblo, Colorado, now stands, had spent the ensuing winter among a few mountain men. His account of the episode is freely sprinkled with the roughness, crudity, callousness to suffering, and ready brutality of the frontier and the mountain men. To him, at first, these men who preceded the settlers seemed to be whites reduced to savagery. But with a second thought denied the more superficial observers, he grew to respect their hardihood, their masculinity, their "quick determination and resolve in peril, fixedness of purpose." Ruxton recounts his own experience of a solitary night of terror, spent crouched under a blanket in a blizzard in the Bayou Salado (now South Park, Colorado), and other similar hardships. Yet hear his summary:

> Still there was something inexpressibly exhilirating in the sensation of positive freedom from all worldly care, and a consequent expansion of the sinews, as it were, of mind and body. . . . Although liable to an accusation of barbarism, I must confess that the very happiest moments of my life have been spent in the wilderness of the Far West; and I never recall but with pleasure . . . my solitary camp in the Bayou Salado, with no friend near me more faithful than my rifle, and no companions more sociable than my good horses and mules, or the attendant coyote . . . Scarcely, however, did I ever wish to change such hours of freedom for all the luxuries of civilized life, and, unnatural and extraordinary as it may appear, yet such is the fascination of the life of the mountain hunter, that I believe not one instance could be adduced of even the most polished and civilised of men, who had once tasted the sweets of its attendant liberty and freedom . . . not regretting the moment when he exchanged it for the monotonous life of the settlements, nor sighing, and sighing again, once more to partake of its pleasures and allurements.[9]

This was, remember, no savage of the European romancers, no "natural man," no American frontiersman degraded by separation from the states, the type of whom Washington Irving observed on his trip to the prairies that you could pay him no greater compliment

[9] George Frederick Ruxton, *Ruxton of the Rockies,* ed. LeRoy R. Hafen, pp. 261–262.

than to persuade him that you had mistaken him for an Indian. This was a cultivated young Englishman. If we could but fathom that strange happiness in retrospect, that complete renunciation of civilization, we might touch the secret of the new geography, the heady wine of freedom, the widespread appeal of the American west. That secret does not lie in learned treatises on the romantic movement in Europe—which, in fact, was itself stimulated by the shock of the new geography—nor on the philosophic antecedents of revolution, but in experience.

The problem, however, was how to translate that experience, as it came forth in journals and diaries, letters and published interviews, reports and descriptions, into literature, into essay, poem, and novel. The new frontiersman needed cleaning up; he needed to be abstracted into a new kind of man, furnished with a point of view and a significance within his New World setting. This task was left for James Fenimore Cooper; and his Preface to a later edition of *The Leather-Stocking Tales* sufficiently summarizes Cooper's blend of romanticism and natural virtue, the hero with the instinctive innocence of nature's solitudes, cleansed by the great out-of-doors of the vices of white or savage:

The idea of delineating a character that possessed little of civilization but its highest principles as they are exhibited in the uneducated, and all of savage life that is not incompatible with these great rules of conduct, is perhaps natural to the situation in which Natty was placed. He is too proud of his origin to sink into the condition of the wild Indian, and too much a man of the woods not to imbibe as much as was at all desirable from his friends and companions. . . . To use his own language, his "gifts" were "white gifts" . . . On the other hand, removed from nearly all the temptations of civilized life . . . his hero was a fit subject to represent the better qualities of both conditions. . . .

[And again] A being removed from the every-day inducements to err, which abound in civilized life, while he retains the best and simplest of his early impressions; who sees God in the forest; hears him in the winds . . . in a word, a being who finds the impress of the Deity in all the works

of nature, without any of the blots produced by the expedients, and passion, and mistakes of man.[10]

Is this not precisely the language of the "natural man" starting
over from experience in the original purity of this new Eden, the
forest? He is not only spared the "expedients" of man, his governments, institutions, social rigidities, but he is even exempted from
man's native passions and errors. He is indeed a new Adam. The
Indian, the man of the forest, confirms his instinct for direct impulse
and courage, the white teaches him reverence without corruption;
but it is the natural setting, the forest, which preserves Natty from
the vices of either. *The Deerslayer* (last to be written in the series,
and perhaps therefore at the peak of the idealization of this Natty
Bumppo figure) places the hero at his most youthful and most
innocent, alone on a forest lake as yet unnamed, lake and forest and
hero all virgin territory, over which, as has been pointed out, it is
usually sunrise, symbol of the fresh promise of the day. The Deerslayer is less a Rousseau primitive than an American innocent, unaware of Europe's guilty past, reared as an orphan in a Moravian
mission, but now alone, relying instinctively on a native simplicity
and purity of motive and his own frontier skills to carry him through
every peril.

Here is a native creation, almost the first in any rounded proportions, a Daniel Boone cleaned up and rarefied, more fictional than
literal, no doubt, but corresponding as had no previous creation to
what America wanted to believe. Many have pointed out the simi-
larities between Natty Bumppo and Boone; but Cooper, we may
say, inaugurated the romanticizing of the new man in fictional form,
amid the native scene. Henry Nash Smith has lucidly shown how
Cooper's hero led by inevitable steps to the Diamond Dicks, the

---

[10] James Fenimore Cooper, *Works,* Preface, I, 4. Any consideration of Cooper's influence on western fiction must be indebted to Henry Nash Smith's *Virgin Land: The
American West as Symbol and Myth.* See also Richard Chase, *The American Novel
and its Tradition,* Chapter III.

invincible gun which sets right basic injustices, and the whole
Hollywood legend; and there is no need to repeat the story here. The
original Natty Bumppo is a purer figure, the new man finally given
body and a habitation. He is neither Yankee trader nor Puritan
psalmsinger, both disliked by Cooper, nor is he a Southern plantation gentleman, nor yet a poor farmer. He exists in his own right,
a personalized simplification of the shock of geography upon the
white strain; and his popularity lingers still, for he is American. In
1917, when America entered World War I on the side of France, a
French orator surprised his American hearers by his fervid toast:
"The spirit of Leather-Stocking is awake!"

As Henry Nash Smith has well indicated, Natty posed, nevertheless, a host of practical queries, for he represented aspirations with a
truly limited future in a rising America. He might be a symbol as
a breaker of new trails and the escape from the hampering traditions
of the past, but what had such a man, solitary and free, guided only
by an instinct for forest paths amid the isolation of an unmapped
wilderness, to say to an industrialized nation? Agriculture, the major
fact in the young United States, levelled the forests about him and
plowed the new prairies. Land laws, game laws, sheriffs, and courts,
pursued him westward and must eventually overtake him. How
could a simple egalitarian code match a rising new classification of
men in terms of education and wealth? And an innocence which
made virtue more natural than vice, the natural religion of the forest, intuitive, semipantheistic, indifferent to ritual or credal differences, noncommunicant, product of the lone individual under the
stars and the silences of the forest tops, how might it survive the
assaults of an aggressive and organized institutionalism? In short,
what prospect had this individual of the frontier save a gradual
elimination? Could there be found an intellectual parallel, capable
of survival within civilization, linked with the native note yet not
dependent on the waning frontier? This topic, nearer to the purpose
of this essay, will occupy us in a further chapter.

The later popularity of the cowboy theme, let us say, owes something also to this legend of man in nature, preserved from the corruptions of the big centers of population, the free individual still capable of living by a private code because his living is set in the solitudes of nature. The cowboy's occupation makes possible this transference; for by necessity he moves about in large areas of open land, is largely a law to himself, is still nomadic in his freedom to roam for his jobs from Texas to Canada. Coupled with a handy skill with a gun and an innate sense of common justice, this occupation was a natural equivalent of the early man in nature, the last symbol of a passing geographical and a consciously felt frontier; the man on horseback, combination of the knight in armor, Natty Bumppo, and the west's own spaciousness.

What does he represent, this modern myth-man, as he appears in the next western film, dusty and alone, alighting with studied unconcern from his horse, the distant spaces in his noncommittal eyes, speaking in monosyllables, alert and wary despite his casual pose, openly armed, though for emergencies only? A ready killer upon provocation, he is no murderer, no badman, since he is a hero; and every American boy is presumably aware of the difference, for he kills only in defense of personal honor or of helpless womanhood. He is, in true frontier fashion, a law unto himself. Yet, though he takes justice into his own hands, it is still the justice of chivalry and honor, and the folk who stand about in the little clapboard town appear to approve of his code, for these sure intuitions as to where justice lies are apparently imbibed in the course of things from the great open spaces, the wide prairies, and the tall mountains.

Certainly this legendary hero of our own cinematic day is not civilized in any parlor sense. If he can read, he is rarely caught at it in the Hollywood versions. He tolerates civilization only for drinks, card games, easy women, and a renewal of provisions. His killings, in the third-rate pictures, need very small provocation, and the bystanders and the heroine turn most casually from the corpse to celebrate his victory. He is wary of women, however, for they threaten his freedom; and domesticity, though he is always politely grateful for kindness from pure hands, is not his goal. So off he rides alone, hinting at distant destinations: El Paso, Tombstone, Virginia City, even Laramie. Book law he ignores unless it is on his side; his religion is simplicity itself, that of swift justice to evildoers and affronters to his manhood, and an occasional generosity to widows and orphans. He is, Robert Warshow calls him in a brief article, "the last gentleman," in the sense that he lives by a code of honor: fair duel and open challenge, no shooting in the back, and the rescue of those in distress.[11] "Fair play," a term said to be untranslatable into other languages, and unknown to the bullies of Nazism, Fascism, and Communism, lingers in the cowboy legend.

Nevertheless, since he is a killer and on his own, his best efforts are tainted with the outlaw stain, and his end is loneliness and melancholy. Inevitably, then, the associations are with the lugubrious songs of "the lone prairie" and the hopeless, yet deeply American, cry of "Don't fence me in." He is the hero of adolescents and immature adults; any man who tried to live by his code in a modern town would be arrested as a common drunk and madman. He shares with boys of fourteen a contempt for washing behind the ears, for girls, and for domestic restraints in general. His Hollywood role, as has frequently been observed, is a strictly determined one, for his audiences, like those of the ancient Greek drama, know the outcome and wait only to see how the hero will behave in the crisis and to share in the triumph of fate and swift justice. As a folk hero, he represents a fading concept drawn from a romanticized past; at least he rises above the blackshirted sadists of a more recent past or the sinister gangsters of our own great cities, toward both of whom he would have felt an instinctive hostility.

His world shrinks and shrinks, until, like the last bison, he has

[11] Robert Warshow, "Movie Chronicle: The Westerner," *Partisan Review,* XXI (March, 1954), 235–238.

nowhere to go, unless to the last Canadian north. Modern transportation brings his farthest horizons next door, and litters them with the refuse of the ubiquitous tourist. His type—nomad, hunter, herder of flocks—has always preceded civilization and cities. He is, alas, but a formula in a third-rate film, as remote as Jason and his Golden Fleece. Only recently has his passing been the subject of a new kind of western, tentatively exploring his significance: *Shane, High Noon, Lonely Are the Brave, The Outcasts.* Even these are nostalgic, and carry no clear hint as to how we may recover the remnants of a lost individualism.

Thus, by steps somewhat too summary, we arrive at a kind of crisis in the American literary scene. The transplanted European has experienced the shock and challenge of a new environment and a new opportunity, the stimulus of freedom and self-reliance, the lure of adventure, risk, and landscapes awaiting exploring. This experience has irresistibly modified his attitude toward his European inheritance, even erased much of it, and made possible a dynamic social and political revolution, whose consequences will echo far in other lands. That political stream possesses its own kind of vitality and makes itself felt in ways that lie outside our present study.

But what of the national hope for a literature commensurate with the new experience? Was that to trickle out in the arid wastes of the west, and the oversimplified legend of the cowboy and the gunman? Or might the American experience be transmuted somehow into a viable literary expression? For the old aspiration to reach the world with a new hope dies hard, even while we smile in the pose of sophistication at its naiveté and its romantic overtones.

We should miss a central point if we so foolishly allowed our theme to fade away in the melodrama of popular entertainment. It is the function of literature to probe to a deeper interpretation of the human scene. Cooper, it appears, was not in the main stream, precisely because he romanticized an idealization, even as in his political papers he lingered with the prejudices of a landed gentry.

To romanticize means to attempt to capture what is not present, either in time or in space, and to do so as a means of escape from a present reality. Its end is not reality, not even a measurable blueprint for the future, which time may vindicate. Here, too, lies a difference. America's vitality has always turned to the future, the potential within a smaller present, the possible not yet realized. Its idealization has not been solely romantic; it has also been dynamic.

There was, then, a still unexploited possibility for American literature: the transmutation of the frontier theme into the figure and metaphor of literary expression. This the New Englander attempted first, sensing in the history of the west a new hope on other fronts than the geographical.

part 2   FRONTIERS OF THOUGHT

The frontiers are not east or west, north or south; but
wherever a man *fronts* a fact.—Henry Thoreau,
A Week on the Concord and Merrimack Rivers

vi. A Native Metaphor Is Born

THE TITLE of this section, "Frontiers of
Thought," was no haphazard choice. It
was suggested, indeed, by one of many
available passages from the writings of Henry Thoreau, in this case
his *A Week on the Concord and Merrimack Rivers,* begun around
1839 and published a decade later. Thoreau wrote:

> The frontiers are not east or west, north or south; but wherever a man
> *fronts* a fact . . . there is an unsettled wilderness . . . between him and the
> setting sun, or farther still, between him and *it.* Let him build himself a log-
> house with the bark on where he is, *fronting IT,* and wage there an old French
> War for seven or seventy years, with Indians and Rangers, or whatever else
> may come between him and the reality, and save his scalp if he can.[1]

Thoreau was a great insister on reality and the original self-experi-
ence, which alone legitimately demands expression, and the italics
are his. Here, with typical Thorovian emphasis and imagery, drawn
from the concreteness of man in the wilderness, Thoreau challenges
his neighbors to come to grips with reality in the realm of human

[1] All quotations from Thoreau are from *Writings of Henry Thoreau,* hereafter referred to as *Writings.* The above passage is from *A Week on the Concord and
Merrimack Rivers,* hereafter referred to as *A Week, Writings,* I, 401.

thought even as their compatriots were being compelled on literal frontiers to confront the hazards and the solitudes of their isolated log huts. The frontier experience, in short, has been absorbed into the imagination of a writer and his total possible public, and has yielded up a new kind of figure, simile and metaphor. The frontier, in the mind of America, is on its way to becoming the natural symbol for resolution, courage, the confrontation of hard realities from which there is no convenient escape, the courage of the individual fighter who can rely on none other for his salvation. A native metaphor is born.

That this metaphor may carry Puritan overtones becomes evident quickly in Thoreau, at least with the ethical corollaries of resisting temptations to ease, accepting no substitute for a personal participation in the drama of salvation, and confronting one's fate directly and without intermediate illusions. Thus Thoreau can make use of an ancient New England law that "every settler who deserted a town for fear of the Indians, should forfeit all his rights therein" to point the parallel for those who "may desert the fertile frontier territories of truth and justice, which are the State's best lands, for fear of far more insignificant foes." [2] So are symbols born, blends, it may be, of new experience and past inheritance, each seeking fresh expression. But it is the new which has furnished the livelier element.

The frontier thus by degrees becomes a thematic metaphor, ready for use. Were these quotations isolated examples only, they might be dismissed as the play of an eccentric. But Thoreau knew his countrymen, and appealed always in his writing to their readiness for his argument and his meaning. He selected his figures and metaphors with care, within the common store of experience, so that all might comprehend him.

How far-reaching was this metaphor of the American frontier? How far did it penetrate into the psychology of a people, and to

[2] *Ibid.*, I, 143.

what extent could it influence the writings of a rising literature? These are queries which we must examine in more detail. But let us consider for a moment the nature of metaphor.

"Man," wrote Emerson in *Nature,* "is an analogist, and studies relations in all things." Emerson himself often strained such relations beyond reason, in his search for what he called "correspondences between natural and spiritual facts." One might say that he did not fully perceive the pitfalls within his own observation, or the subtle temptations that hover about reliance on the analogy. Yet Emerson was not without his own shrewdness in such matters, as witness a remark in "The Poet":

Here is the difference betwixt the poet and the mystic, that the last nails a symbol to one sense, which was a true sense for a moment, but soon becomes old and false. For all symbols are fluxional; all language is vehicular and transitive, and is good, as ferries and horses are, for conveyance, not as farms and houses are, for homestead. Mysticism consists in the mistake of an accidental and individual symbol for a universal one.

Emerson's advice to the mystic is "Let us have a little algebra"; that is, let us recognize the nature of a symbol as an x to aid us toward the larger solution. The symbol, says Emerson, can become "too stark and solid, and . . . at last nothing but an excess of the organ of language."[3] Thoreau, as is usual, goes more bluntly and directly to the matter, saying in *Walden,* "We are in danger of forgetting the language which all things and events speak without metaphor, which alone is copious and standard."[4] These writers exhibit thus a certain consistency in their approach to metaphors; and if they appear to draw often on the similes of nature, it is, as Thoreau says, that "these things speak without metaphor," directly. Long later we shall find a major American poet, Wallace Stevens, echoing Thoreau here.

[3] Ralph Waldo Emerson, "The Poet," *Works,* III, 37.
[4] Thoreau, *Walden, Writings,* II, 174.

A metaphor, an analogy, makes its appeal insofar as it yields intellectual and emotional satisfaction, adds illumination to an idea, or provides the illusion of a convincing argument. Yet a metaphor, as Emerson, to his credit, was striving to say in *Nature,* does not begin in myth but in natural fact. One of its feet must be planted on the soil of daily experience, even if the other, to borrow the overheated words of an orator pursuing liberty, point triumphantly to the skies. Every metaphor risks its absurdity, even madness.

For a metaphor begins either in something concrete, the sum of repeated experience, which has suggested the leap into the abstraction of a generalization; or it arises from the gropings of some previously evolved abstraction, some rarefied concept, which feels the necessity for support and so grasps at the illumination of a comparison with the concrete, something within the repetitions of experience. In either case, the concrete has given sinews to the metaphor. Thus far the metaphor may be useful, and there is no need to scorn its contribution. The illusory element, the danger, the madness, enters when the abstracted portion is assumed to be proved, to be more valid than the concrete base, or when the metaphor begins to breed its own litter of analogies and new metaphors, each farther removed from the corrections of experience. For experience always awaits in the wings to prompt the correctives and to restore sanity.

The successful metaphor tends to become bolder and to feed upon its own success. Once accepted as a useful illumination, it may swell by monstrous degrees, insisting on a life apart or on a total loyalty to its supposed finality, and without regard to the ensuing inconsistencies and the sacrifice of judgment. Nations have risen and fallen around the gigantism of a metaphor which may have begun in an obvious need for heroism, unity, or action, but which has ended in the madness of denying all that would restrain its exaggeration. Men are "classified" on the analogy of plants and animals; nations are frozen into the stereotypes of bears, bulls, cocks, and apes; the complexities of international relations are reduced to the metaphor of a

football field with "gains" and victories. A swastika provokes to
paranoic unity and the color red to schizoid confusions of loyalties.
What may have originated in the natural resistance of man or of
men to being enslaved or defeated slides by degrees into the myth of
a unique virtue and prowess, a legend of eternal rightness and in-
vincibility, the protection of a special deity, and the madness of a
mission to impose oneself or one's national will upon others—and
Nemesis stirs at last to prepare the final act. Fortunately, however,
metaphors and analogies, being our daily fare, are as often used but
lightly, picked up and tossed aside as their flicker of usefulness is
exhausted. By their very number they serve to counteract one another; and the common sense of man retains an instinctive humor in
its awareness of their limitations.

Inevitably the frontier emerged as a favored American metaphor,
embedded as it was in two or three centuries of history, and thus the
most available of symbols for courage, self-reliance, survival against
odds, and the individual on his own. Our past had demanded energy
and resolution commensurate with great mountains and rivers and
expansive plains. If in time that frontier would be traversed and
reduced in area, or for the majority would pass beyond the day of
personal experience and melt into legend, the symbol would nevertheless remain, to proliferate in imaginative corollaries.

The frontiersman himself was, indeed, "ahistorical" and unin-
volved in the historical past. This is but a statement of fact, an
inevitable fact, and not the theme for a lecture on his limitations
and crudities. He could scarcely be frontiersman and parlor philosopher at the same time. His philosophy was developed out of his
experience, and hence valued resolution and readiness to act above
subtleties in argument. Being uncouth and out of his element in an
urban setting, he took his revenge by magnifying his own virtues.
But these are considerations not germane at the moment to our query,
which is how his virtues might find a counterpart in the more
literate part of America. Translate them, that is, into the terms of an

Emerson, Thoreau, or Whitman, and we become at once aware that
they suggest precisely what they, in fact, became, the symbols of an
assertion of individuality and self-reliance in more metaphysical
terms, but terms rooted still in experience. In the ancient dichotomy
between thinkers, that of traditional "values" versus the ahistorical
right to begin over with a new evaluation forced by new experience,
the American would be on the side of the experiential, the pragmatic, the open horizons of the explorer. Further, a native literature
must be born of wrestling with the direct and native experience as
against a literature derivative merely from the past. There may be,
that is, as much of Edwards, Franklin, and the Concord farms in
Emerson as of Schiller and Plotinus, more in Thoreau of Johnny
Appleseed than of Buddha or Calvin.[5]

Emerson, for all his library bookishness—and who has found convincing "sources" for Emerson?—insisted with his whole antinomian
inheritance that education was the power of fact over words, of
nature and the native experience over convention. Far from saying,
"I owe my all to Plato or Plotinus," or "I shall seek out a German
idealist and become a disciple," Emerson urged the American
scholar to set himself up as a contrast to "the book-learned class,
who value books, as such; not as related to nature and the human
constitution." Surely, then, a considerable portion of the American
effort, between roughly 1820 and 1860, to create a native literature
had to be devoted to an exploration of its own resources, the implications of its own experience and knowledge, whose concrete base
was a common possession.

[5] "The three sources [of Transcendentalism]," says a handbook (R. W. Horton and
H. W. Edwards, *Backgrounds of American Literary Thought,* p. 112), ". . . are neo-
Platonism, German idealist philosophy, and certain Eastern mystical writings." Granted
that the parallels and the links exist, is there to be no mention of a native impulse?
Are these true "sources," pertinent for comparison, or evidences of American eclecticism? Or were they stimulants to a native restlessness with the old Puritan-European
orthodoxy, no longer viable in the American setting—a suggestion, perhaps, that by
analogy, the native experience might be examined for its own grain of a unique
significance?

Obviously it will not do to ignore the steady stream of cultural influences from Europe from the time of the first settlements, the importation of books and men, the Renaissance pattern of education in the colleges, the easily available evidence that the colonies were European colonies still, and long remained so in the growing centers on the Atlantic coast. Nevertheless, the other side likewise imposes its evidence upon us: the rising awareness of a new way of viewing life, the consciousness of a new kind of man and society, fruits of a new experience. "The nervous, rocky West," wrote Emerson in 1844, "is intruding a new and continental element into the national mind, and we shall yet have an American genius." [6] There it was in one sentence. And in the *Democratic Review* of 1842 we may read: "Probably no other civilized nation has at any period . . . so completely thrown off its allegiance to the past . . . ; the whole essay of our national life and legislation has been a prolonged protest against the dominion of antiquity in every form whatsoever." [7] Protest against the tyranny of the past, the search for a native voice, these are the concomitants of the new experience and the new awareness.

At an even earlier date, before Emerson and Thoreau, before Melville's "strike through the mask," and Whitman's "Song of Myself," Alexis de Tocqueville, visiting America around 1831 to 1832, made much of the American preference for individual experience and its mistrust of ready-made systems. His Book II opens with a list of major American tendencies: to evade system and habit, to accept tradition only as information, to seek the reason of things for and in oneself, to strike through form to substance, in sum, to exhibit the dominant trait of appealing each problem "to the individual effort of his own understanding." [8]

We should keep these characteristics in mind when we approach any study of our mid-period, the first true flowering of American

---

[6] Emerson, "The Young American," *Works,* I, 349.

[7] Quoted by R. W. B. Lewis, *The American Adam,* p. 159.

[8] Alexis de Tocqueville, *Democracy in America,* ed. Phillips Bradley, II, 3–4.

literature before the war that rent the states and muffled the optimism of the new republic. American scholarship increasingly seeks some national pattern within our fluid history, and numerous excellent studies have greatly augmented our understanding. In the hands of some lesser writers, beginners in the search, there has been a tendency to lean heavily on the solemn word "myth," or to use it loosely and in the wrong direction, as if myth preceded the hard facts of living or as if the average pragmatic man sought by his experience to substantiate some hoary myth. Where do these myth seekers assume myths to have originated in the first place? The Mayans built pyramids without knowledge of Egyptian labors—and even if they had not, where did the Egyptians get their knowledge?—precisely because the first sheepherder who piled up stones on some lonely height could not without mortar erect a vertical tower. And if one discovers upon a hilltop in the west a primitive throne erected by some Navajo herdsman out of the natural slabs that lie about, with back and sides high and impressive and the whole facing the east, he needs no myth of ancient sun worship to recognize that the prevailing winds are from the west and the shelter a pragmatic convenience.

When one reads that the settlement of the Ohio-Mississippi basin was all but spawned by "the myth of the Garden of Eden," he need not lose his head. The fact is that to one nurtured on the rocky hillsides of New England, the promise of soil ten feet deep without rocks was heartening news to weary muscles and tightened purses. And if the emigrant, trying to convey back home the grateful note of a new promise, made use of a familiar vocabulary in phrases like "garden of Eden," and "paradise," he but drew on his limited resources without thought of Jungian overtones, even as the original phrase no doubt recorded some similar transfer to a fertile river basin. The terms are very old and very familiar; one recalls old John of Gaunt's dying speech in *Richard II* and his tribute to England: "this other Eden, demi-paradise . . . the envy of less happier lands."

Other youthful writers manage to convey a tone of rebuke to the frontiersman because he somehow failed to remember the Promethean myth and its lesson of punishment for self-assertion over humbleness and pride in accomplishment. Is this some curious sublimation of the exhorting impulse disguising itself behind a Greek myth? The Promethean legend carried in America the Shelleyean overtones of revolt against the static past. The fact is, however, that the frontiersman's very exaggeration and assertiveness was but proof of the necessity of a self-image of hardihood, courage, and resourcefulness as a bulwark against the severity of his experience and the limitations of his powers in the face of raw nature. His boasting, like that in all primitive literature, whether by Homer or Beowulf, is but a product of his major concern, survival against odds. In America it served, too, as a warning to the weak and faint-hearted to stay at home, nursing their timidities. Would these moralizers have had the pioneer grow sick with apprehension and turn back to the older, more familiar refuges, built for him by bolder men? Whatever its hidden symbolism, Captain Ahab's language of encouragement to his crew to persist in courage had also its practical counterpart on a thousand raw frontiers.

Perhaps we need, when considering the impact of the American frontier on a native literature, a new theory of books, comparable to Emerson's view in "The American Scholar." Do books precede and determine history; or are they, rather, thrown off like fruits from the tree to celebrate the seasonal changes in the climate of opinion and event, and so return to earth to fertilize the next growths? Do metaphors arise apart from experience, or do they but record the searing impact of experience to suggest to the emergent mind the parallels for an order sought? Whether books instigate history or record it, or do both, they do provide convenient clues to the progress of history. In either case, they also permit the query to take the form of how and why they come into being.

Human experience, within any given space and period of time,

86

tends to crystallize into habits both physical and mental, which in
turn become traditions, and, their origins being gradually lost or
obscured, are treated as legend, myth, belief, assumptions unexamined. Society, relaxing in the illusion of permanence and stability,
celebrates the whole complex by means of "history," the appeal to
a peculiar destiny in events leading to the stable moment, even
by a credo of rightness, of inevitability that brooks no questioning.
The books which summarize these happy eras, even as Dante spoke
for an age and Locke justified a *fait accompli,* are valued as "proofs"
of that rightness, that destiny.

But few things in history prove to be eternal. Some new shock
introduces new strains, new queries, new obstacles to relaxation;
the least that can happen is some new readjustment, some loss of the
past; and the worst may be the rise of superheated passions, fac-
tions, and civil wars in which the old is destroyed or vitally changed
even if the pretended victors have defended the old.

Herein a book may synthesize the elements of the struggle on
one side or another, may permit of some pause for reflection, or may
hasten action. But it is still a product of factors long at work, so that
it never can be seen as sole determinant in the events that follow.
And what, after all, tests its validity or lack of validity but the subsequent record of experience? Yet experience is no static thing; it
too shifts with setting and time and pressures. The lesson would
seem to favor flexibility, and even the consultation of experience as
at least a reinforcement of abstract philosophizing, a saving grace
amid the crumbling temples to the past.

At any rate, the American past by the mid-1830's was fully two
centuries old; and whether the new nation was a product of selec-
tive forces from the European social, economic, and religious unrest,
or of the impact of new freedoms and opportunities upon these
selected émigrés, something new was emerging, "a fact new to the
world," De Tocqueville surmised, "a fact that the imagination strives

in vain to grasp." [9] It was this new fact that American writers must wrestle with, sooner or later, in their own and not in borrowed terms. It was this new fact that they cultivated in pride and expanded by metaphor and simile into the rudiments of a philosophy for the individual and his inherent meaning.

[9] *Ibid.*, I, 452.

vii. Religion on the Frontier

RELIGION on the western frontier increasingly took on the pattern of its environment, the individualism and optimism, the casual indifference to old, inherited forms, the assertion of a new beginning, even if with these the crudities of an aggressive evangelism accompanied often by anti-intellectualism. Thus we find the early Campbellite preacher Walter Scott calling for "a *new* religion and a *new* society in a *new* world," within which every man will be his own conscience and his own interpreter of the Scriptures as they may correspond to his daily living. Then, Scott says, sectarianism will disappear. Scott was characterized by a fellow preacher in vigorous, if crude, frontier language as the first man in America "who took the old field-notes of the apostles and run [sic] the original survey, beginning at Jerusalem." However earthy the language, the sense of it paralleled the more secular, more literate, explorations of the Transcendentalists and their contemporaries. To Scott, "Everything in old society, nearly, that is truly desirable is royal or aristocratic; the people cannot reach it; it belongs, if it is good, to the rich; if bad, to the poor." [1]

[1] Scott is quoted in John A. Kouwenhoven, *Made in America,* p. 136.

Here frontier religion parallels the political curve from theocratic authority to federalism to Jacksonian democracy. Frontier religion came with the second wave of settlement, not the first. But it tended to insist, like its environment, on the individual's own testimony as superseding that of any other for him, the personal experience, the conversion which none could perform for him and which no outward conformities could render valid. Here again is De Tocqueville's dominant character of the American, his appeal "to the individual effort of his own understanding."

Without doubt, much was owing to the impetus already supplied from the Pietist immigrants from northern Europe; but frontier evangelism was America's own invention. Often overlooked is the fact that American Protestantism takes two forms, more sharply in evidence in the European sources: one, that of the old scholastic disputations, argument, reasoning within the frame of theology, such as made the first Protestant literature of the Calvinist strain almost undistinguishable from the Catholic tradition of theological exposition; the other, the Pietist strain which, in its extremes, eschewed all learned debate, all forms and rituals, in the name of a simple inner experience. The latter found the more ready response on the frontier. The Puritan-Presbyterian tradition, more conservative, maintained the three-hour sermons of logical form and substance, the required education of the clergy, and the spread of institutions of learning.

Yet the antinomian groups were numerous—Quaker, Baptist, German Pietist, frontier Methodist, frontier revivalists of whatever peculiar persuasion—each in its degree denying the authority of the past and its institutions, each acting as a disintegrating factor for older patterns, and as encouragement in the direction of a more complete individualism. And from the premise of the individual's private determination of the authenticity of his own conversion, his salvation by inner conviction only, followed inevitably the decay of church as an institutional authority, the withdrawal of the already isolated

frontiersman from the old ties of institutional direction or instruction, the lonely Bible reader in the winter fastnesses of New England,
from whence flowered a host of "Come-Outers," or the semipagan
on the distant frontier.

There followed also the tolerance of members of other groups
who shared a common experience of profession of faith without sec-
tarian distinction, and whose individual testimony was sufficient
evidence of acceptance, with no great concern over minor variations.
The process is at work early, as early as the New England protest
against the Mather oligarchy, the unavoidable relaxation of Puritan
rigidities as population increased and was mingled with newcomers
indifferent to the old faith, the Great Awakening with its stress on
the individual experience and testimony, the easy crossing of de-
nominational lines, and, by the time of the Revolution, the determined drive against disenfranchisement on religious grounds. Traditional theology, official dogma, formal instruction, literacy become
less and less the rule. Churches on the frontier became a regrouping
in response to the new levelling and the scattered social contacts,
and without overmuch concern for the older forms.

Even the pervading democracy of the "saved," the social levelling
which crosses ancient loyalties, political or religious, induced a general tolerance of most sects. And if Quaker and Pietist refused military obligations in the name of their faiths, so, too, did the frontier
take a casual attitude toward a government too remote to exercise
its pressures, too weak to enforce its laws on the edges of civilization. All in all, the whole pattern of frontier living, including the
general absence of religion in any formal sense, and its familiarity
with the religions of evangelism, occasional meetings, and public
conversions, encouraged religious separatism from a historical past
and the usual reliance on self, individual experience, and private
conscience.

Much of this story, however, appears to take place apart from
the literary record. Here we deal, instead, with romanticism and

transcendentalism; and the majority of American writers of larger
fame appear to have been deistic in temper or noncommital as to
religious affiliations. Bryant's daughter, for example, said she was
never quite sure what her father's beliefs were; and the same might
have been said of many others. The frontier pattern for fiction is
set by Cooper, not by the evangelists, and is not without its echoes
in later writers.

Cooper's simple, taciturn, and natural son of the forest, it will be
recalled, remained innocent so long as he avoided the "settlements."
His heroic qualities were formed in solitude and by the necessities
of self-reliance: "in the solitudes of the West," to borrow Emerson's
phrase, "where a man is made a hero by the varied emergencies." [2]
Hero or not, the frontiersman was essentially rootless. He camped
where he paused, under trees or open sky; he built a simple, one-
roomed shelter if he paused for dwelling, looking to better himself
one day by his own efforts, not by an inheritance; he moved again,
not to a new home, but to new lands still awaiting map and sur-
veyor, axe and plow; he was not "gathered unto his fathers," but,
in Bryant's phrase, returned "to mix forever with the elements." His
innocence, if such it was, was that of the fresh horizons with each
new morning and the twinkling of the unobstructed stars with each
evening.

Translate this image of the rootless man into symbols for Emerson's "Man Thinking" and the parallels unfold. The American
thinker, as Emerson envisages him in all his unique newness, remains innocent and freshly perceptive so long as he avoids the
settled systems of the past, so long as he inhabits, in Emerson's own
phrase, "the Western lands of the mind," so long as he keeps with
Melville's Bulkington "the open independence of her [the soul's]
sea." These parallels we shall explore further in the next chapters.

The famous Turner thesis of the "return to primitive conditions

---

[2] Emerson, "Fortune of the Republic," *Works,* XI, 416.

on a continually advancing line" of frontier, from which experience evolve "the forces dominating American character," is too narrowly political and economic for the purposes of literary analogy. On the one hand it minimizes the tendency of the west (a tendency reflected more particularly in literature) to repeat the familiar materials of the past or to import from the farther east, and on the other it makes little mention of the blend of past and present and the insistent problem of language which must always enter into the creation of literature. Language by its repetitive nature is implicit with tradition, and any new reaching out for self-expression will assume uncertain shapes, tentative and timid. At times this reaching will be scarcely conscious of its groping function, at other times it may be overly aggressive in its rejection of the past. Nevertheless, every phase of American life will feel the pull of a new need for expression, will be touched by the silent, encompassing wilderness and the free breezes that blow in from the west.

Even so austere a figure as Jonathan Edwards, one may be surprised to discover, will illustrate something of this frontier innocence and this reference to self-trust. Sensitive in the extreme to the pressures of being upon body and mind, he reveals in rare moments a personal response to his environment. Born on the sparsely inhabited western Massachusetts frontier, he early found "particular secret places of my own in the woods," [3] from which unbookish religious analogies might flow. "The fields and woods," he writes, "seem to rejoice, and how joyful do the birds seem to be in it. How much a resemblance is there of every grace in the field covered with plants and flowers when the sun shines serenely and undisturbedly upon them." Men, even the most miserable, he remarks, love life, "because they cannot bear to lose sight of such a beautiful and lovely

[3] "Personal Narrative" in *Representative Selections from Jonathan Edwards,* eds. Clarence H. Fause and Thomas N. Johnson, p. 57.

world." [4] Who would normally assign such phrases to Jonathan Edwards? And how delightfully full of natural observation is the precocious essay from the boy of thirteen on the habits of the spider.

Such passages are the language of solitude in nature, not that of Calvin's *Institutes;* and excursions such as these, it may well be, led Edwards to his essay on "A Divine and Supernatural Light," that essay so closely akin to the Quaker privacy with its emphasis on the "immediately given," to be reached "by a kind of intuitive and immediate evidence" (the words are the words of Edwards), the whole experience owing little to secondary causes, priest, Bible, or institution; for these others, precisely like books for Emerson's scholar, were but aids for the scholar's or the worshipper's lesser moments. This is not the language of those belated medievalists John Winthrop or John Cotton, or even that of the medieval mystics; it is that of a boy and man thrown upon his own solitary resources, seeking corroboration for his reflections in his own experience.

However, this is but one side of Edwards. Another and less native influence was even more deeply at work upon him; and herein lies, perhaps, a hint for a resolution of that apparent contradiction between the European inheritance and American independency. That resolution lies in the freedom of the American to welcome the new and the old from Europe, to examine the inheritance anew in the light of its adaptability to the present situation and to one's own reflection. Such was the strength of the American revolutionists in politics—to have given the abstract speculations of European philosophers a concrete and a modified and practical reality.

Few scholars today accept the customary cliché on Edwards, that he was simply the last defender of a waning Calvinism. He was that, but much more—and here we are all indebted to the penetrating

---

[4] Jonathan Edwards, "Images or Shadows of Divine Things," quoted in Norman Foerster, *American Poetry and Prose*, 4th ed., I, 90.

studies of Perry Miller—because he set about his task by means of a major effort to comprehend the significance of the newer currents of a seventeenth- and eighteenth-century rationalism, specifically the new science of Sir Isaac Newton and John Locke. These British figures are deeply involved in any consideration of eighteenth-century American thinking; but to Edwards was left the effort to reconcile the old with the new. The happier American solution was to accept the new in its superficial meaning without undue concern about the old. Such was Benjamin Franklin's adjustment.

By his own account, Edwards, as a boy of fourteen in his second year at Yale, had been profoundly impressed by the psychology of John Locke, which taught that all knowledge proceeded from the concrete, sensory experience alone. Edwards, like many Puritans and their descendants, possessed a very genuine interest in practical science. Had his lot been cast in England or France, he might well have turned into a speculative thinker in the newer mode. Confined, however, to the frontiers of New England, destined by ancestry and environment to the pulpit, he subjugated this new interest to theology and to speculations therein of a complex sort.

A plausible case might be made for the thesis that the influence of Locke alone sufficed to lead Edwards to his experiments with the Great Awakening, that revival movement which, ironically enough, undermined the very Calvinism which he sought to preserve. For if the individual's inner knowledge arose only from the sensory impact of outward stimuli, the religious experience must have a similar source. The stimuli to conversion remained therefore to be discovered. And if the inner conviction of "grace" was the final evidence of the individual's salvation, and the individual's own assertion that he had known the "experience" the inescapable starting point for any outward examination, what became of the mysteries of "election," predestination, and theocratic control? Professor Miller has called attention to the high incidence of visual imagery in Edwards' sermons, as if he endeavored by such means to assault the inner citadels of emotion and conversion and to plant the initial stimuli to reflection. It was as if Edwards had anticipated William James in his argument that to assume the muscular stance of a powerful emotion was to provoke the appropriate feeling. The analogies of nature's calm serenity, because it rebelled not to the laws of the universe, and of man's wretchedness because he offered rebellion, sufficed to launch American revivalism and to provide Edwards with a laboratory of human emotions. He was the first American psychologist of religious behavior, and that because, like any scientist, he turned to experiential data.

If we follow Professor Miller's analysis,[5] Edwards, it would appear, had reflected deeply on Newton's atomistic cosmogony and the consequences for a universe thoroughly and mechanistically "predestined" by unalterable mathematical laws. Here, too, might be a logical way to reinforce Calvinism; for, if one accepted without question Newton's atomistic machine (Newton himself, it may be recalled, wavered before his own theory, hesitating to push it to its full Lucretian implications), there remained only the problem of a Creator to resolve. Given a Creator whose universe was so ordered, the rest was obvious: the universe was predicated, predestined from the beginning, running by fixed laws which no man could set aside. If this were true of the physical universe, by analogy it should be no less true of the moral universe—the eighteenth century, it must be remembered, made no sharp distinction between mathematical, physical, philosophic, or moral "law," assuming the universe to be of one piece within the great chain of being. Man's mind had only to accept the fact of universal "law" and conform to the consequences, since he could change nothing and could find peace only in a total submission. Thus Edwards could conjure up from the new science a strong weapon to demonstrate the inevitable submis-

[5] Any student of Edwards must be indebted to Perry Miller's *Jonathan Edwards;* see also Miller's *Errand into the Wilderness* for the essay entitled "From Edwards to Emerson."

sion of the human will to the eternal will, unrelieved even by the evolutionary prospect of a later generation.

But Edwards' speculations languished in unpublished notes, and the currents of America moved from such complexities to a new optimism and a new individualism that found in nature's fixed laws ammunition for a new hope, a new revolt against old forms and institutions, and a new thesis of confidence in the natural man. Man, granted reason by a benevolent Creator, had but to search out the laws of the universe and contemplate a future of science applied to man's relief and of goodness founded on logical premises. Edwards was left far behind.

Yet there is at least a plausible link between Edwards' introspective response to nature and Emerson's essay *Nature;* and it is interesting to note that the Unitarian Channing found in Edwards overtones of a kind of nature pantheism. The link, however, lay in the woods and streams and fields of rural New England, symbols for the solitary reflections of sober youth. Neither Edwards nor Emerson approved of the equation of religion with the emotional extremes of frontier revivalism. Yet each reflected his counterpart of the same forces which made the American carry his revolt from the past to the further limits of individualism.

viii. Affirm and Construct—Emerson and Thoreau

RALPH WALDO EMERSON had long been groping toward a resolution of the conflicts implicit within the new era as well as within himself. His roots were deep in New England and he rejoiced in that inheritance, especially as it had engendered habits of plain living and high thinking, independency of mind, and no great concern at the prospect of nonconformity. At the same time, a Puritan soberness touched his revolt with a stubborn passion to "construct," to formulate a new idealism that might serve his countrymen in their search for a national meaning and mission. As an American, Emerson claimed full freedom to think afresh, to restore optimism, and to find a base for new hopes.

This is not the place to pretend a study of the whole Emerson, since our purpose is chiefly to trace what there may be of the American experience in his similes and metaphors and in his significance. That his central drive was a need to explore to the fullest extent the potential that lay within each human being and that this drive carried with it a new assertion of independency from the burden of past opinion goes without argument. Further, that in this ac-

ceptance of the risks of private intuition lay a major source for
Emerson's impact and his originality seems scarcely to be denied.
Few men saw so clearly the risks and plunged so boldly into the
experiment. These were the elements: resistance to the past and
the formulation of a philosophy of self-reliance.

"Much," said Emerson, "was to be resisted, much was to be got
rid of . . . before they could begin to affirm and to construct." [1]
Emerson did not say "reconstruct," neither did he say "overhaul"
or "readjust." His aim was to construct from the base up and to
find the structural materials for the new edifice in the individual's
own intuitions, in the national experience, in nature, in the fresh
frontiers of thought and insight from within.

Emerson, always a prodigious reader, was well acquainted with
the philosophers of the past and the present, nor was his theme without its international overtones. Yet Emerson, returning from his first
trip to Europe in 1833, recorded in his *Journal* (September 1, 1833)
that he was "comforted and confirmed in my convictions . . . I shall
judge more justly, less timidly, of wise men forevermore." In last
analysis, all was to be tried in the crucible of one's own judgment,
one's own reflection. Emerson's American quality lay in the very
incompleteness of his thought, his failure to construct a compre-
hensive philosophic system; it lay, that is, in the application of the
"open society" and confidence in the future to the world of mind
and belief. The more he knew of old and new intellectual "systems,"
the more he continued to affirm the right of the mind to leave all
open for fresh insights. He was thus, as many affirmed, the friend
of seekers; he was also anathema to those who staked all on a closed
system.

The early nineteenth century was an invigorating climate in
which to be alive. The word "freedom" was in the air, troubled, to
be sure, by the terrible inconsistency of human slavery, but in the

---

[1] Emerson, "New England Reformers," *Works*, III, 248.

air, nevertheless, as men advanced westward. Resistance to the dead past, boundless confidence in the future, these were the common note. Mark Twain, who knew the westward pull as did few others, suggested that when the American reached heaven, his first query would be, "Which way West?" Thoreau phrased it more adequately: "When I go out of my house for a walk . . . my needle . . . always settles between west and south-southwest. . . . Eastward I go only by force; but westward I go free. . . . I must walk toward Oregon, and not toward Europe." [2] Nor was Thoreau blind to the intellectual overtones of his preference. Even Hawthorne, distrustful of the Transcendentalists, joined the chorus, in *The House of the Seven Gables,* with Holgrave's outburst against the dead weight of the past: that dead judges determine our decisions, dead men's books supply our thoughts, men long dead have frozen our creeds, and old families and old institutions stand blocking the living renewal in the present. Thoreau agreed in essence: "In my short experience of human life," he wrote, "the *outward* obstacles . . . have not been living men, but the institutions of the dead." [3] The counterpart was Emerson's constant protest against the tyranny of "externals."

The same theme carried over into the territory of literary creativity. Who does not recall Emerson's brave summons to a literary independence in 1837: "We have listened too long to the courtly muses of Europe . . . The millions around us cannot always be fed on the sere remains of foreign harvests." [4] Or Thoreau's "The Atlantic is a Lethean stream, in our passage over which we have had opportunity to forget the Old World and its institutions";[5] or Whitman's Americans "who have left all feudal processes and poems behind them, and assumed the poems and processes of Democracy." [6]

[2] Thoreau, "Walking," *Writings,* IX, 265–266.
[3] Thoreau, "A Week," *ibid.,* I, 167.
[4] Emerson's concluding paragraph in "The American Scholar," *Works,* I, 113.
[5] Thoreau, "Walking," *Writings,* IX, 267.
[6] Walt Whitman, "By Blue Ontario's Shore," *Leaves of Grass,* ed. Emory Holloway, p. 293.

MIDDLEBURY COLLEGE LIBRARY

Such defiance of the dead past was a part of the stimulation of freedom; but the problem, as in all revolutions, lay in Emerson's "affirm and construct." Having cleared the ground of the accumulated rubbish, out of what materials would these iconoclasts construct their new Utopia, their new Zion? They would look, obviously, to the new freedoms within our political and social institutions, the inspiration and promise of an apparently inexhaustible frontier, the promise of a mobile population and industry and a rising prosperity. But chiefly, if they were truly concerned for a native art and literature, they would welcome the freedom to examine all things anew in the light of a fresh and personal experience. Such would seem the logical deduction. Scorning a national materialism, as Emerson and Thoreau professed to do, they must seek the ideal in a new vision of the national setting and opportunity, even of nature as guide, tutor, and pristine inspiration for the intuitions and insights of the solitary genius, withdrawn from social conformities to live by an inner light. And like the old minister in Oliver Wendell Holmes' *Elsie Venner* who "went so far in defence of the rights of man that he put his foot into several heresies," they would shock their contemporaries by their conclusions. But the thunder against them for heresies would be no sufficient shield against their persuasiveness, for the tide was in their favor, and the voices were those of a needful reassertion of the eternal right of youth to re-examine the past and to adjust present opinion to present demands.

In this national revaluation Emerson took a leading part. Overtly indifferent to conformities, he strove again and again to find a base for new affirmations, looking both to individual intuitions and to nature's universal laws as grasped by the same intuition. It was not necessary for him to deny the validity of many older values; on the contrary, he sought to reaffirm them on the solider ground of human experience, reavailable to each individual who would but look about and within and reflect on the significance of what he found. What

Emerson did was to reject the old bases as finalities, to seek new bases conformable to the American experience, and to leave the door open for the grain of truth within any human experience and the systems built thereon. In his effort he drew consciously on the corollaries of the American experience and on the frontier. "Here," he pictures the frontiersman as saying, "here I shall take leave to breathe and think freely. If you do not like it, if you molest me, I can cross the brook and plant a new state out of reach of anything but squirrels and wild pigeons." [7]

But what if squirrels and pigeons offer no intellectual fare; and what if the solitude cut one off from human society; or what if society come again and still again to one's remote cabin door? The answer was to be found in a new definition of solitude, the inner solitude and self-reliance of genius. To Emerson this genius is not for the rare individual; it is, democratically, each man's unique potential, his inner gifts by the light of which he may know, not borrow—or, if borrowing, may test—at least his fragment of the eternal wisdom of nature.

But "nature" means something more than stirring scenery, to which Emerson's personal response would seem to have been rather mild and vague; it means the cosmic unity, the "correspondences" for which nature is but an endlessly varied symbol and metaphor. All men recognize their dependency on nature in the physical realm; they need but read from this universal reservoir of knowledge the deeper lessons of existence. But to read these lessons it is necessary to withdraw from the conventional world about one, where all tends to harden into custom and habit. "You will always find those," says Emerson, "who think they know what is your duty better than you know it. It is easy in the world to live after the world's opinion; it is easy in solitude to live after one's own; but the great man is he who in the midst of the crowd keeps with perfect sweetness the

[7] Emerson, "Boston," *Works*, XII, 102.

independence of solitude." [8] This solution is not only the balance between complete withdrawal from society and being lost in the lowest common denominator of the ways of the crowd; it is also at last the frontier independence come to the urban setting, the transfer of the external solitude to the inner sweetness of self-reliance. The American of any environment may thus assert the same freedom from the world's pressure and the same privilege of self-judgment, for solitude becomes now a state of mind rather than an accident of geography. It is, admittedly, the solution of the bookish man in his private library; but it goes deeper than that, for it is likewise the necessity of the creative artist everywhere.

It is not without significance, then, that Emerson's first published writing should have been entitled *Nature,* nor that its base, despite its over-all idealism, should be essentially and even inevitably Lockean. Emerson, as Unitarian in ancestry and first profession, was, that is, not so much averse to the Lockean base in experience and reason as he was in protest against its apparent finality and its stopping short of something more than the mechanical base. Seeking to step out of "this icehouse of Unitarianism," he nevertheless does not abandon the element of rationalism in his inheritance. Throughout the essay he pursues an organic scheme, with analogies from plant life, and persistently endeavors to begin each time with a concrete base. Wearied today by Emerson's perpetual abstractions and his facile leaps from fact to idealism, echoes both of his recent emancipation from the pulpit, we tend to overlook how his intuitions anticipate a later evolutionary view and the interrelationship of all things, and how regularly he endeavors to maintain the concrete base in experience and nature.

"Nature," as has been remarked above, is, or has long been, a multipurpose word. Used as loosely synonymous with landscape, or with Wordsworth's vaguely benign presence, it had but recently

---

[8] Emerson, "Self-Reliance," *ibid.,* II, 55.

become a romantic addition to the vocabulary. An older connotation of "natural depravity," the Puritan "liberty to do evil," Emerson shunned. Between the two lay the eighteenth-century "nature and nature's laws" within a mathematically ordered universe, in which man, as "endowed by nature and nature's God" with reason and with certain innate liberties, might adjust his social, political, and moral behavior to the universal laws in such a way as to lend them the order and durability of scientific laws. What was inherently right could hardly be unreasonable or contrary to the universal laws behind the observable universe; and the road to such stability could only be discovered, not invented, by the experience and judgment of rational men at their best. Such was the language of Franklin, Jefferson, Paine, Madison, Freneau, Ethan Allen, and others; such were the implications of the opening words of the Declaration of Independence; and such were the overtones of eighteenth-century liberty, tolerance, humanitarianism, and education, as well as of the inherent rights of man as a rational being. This general climate of opinion (an eighteenth-century phrase) had tempted Jonathan Edwards to seek a semiscientific buttress for predestination. The longer range effect was, however, to undermine a rigid determinism and to substitute the hopefulness of progress by the use of reason and the route of cooperation with nature's essentially beneficent laws. America supplied the setting and the evidence of progress to support the plan.

Emerson, for all his romantic note, retains more than a little of this eighteenth-century rationalism in his first essay. His radicalism in it lay in his resolve to see men and morals in organic terms, evolving from natural forces and capable of endless improvement as men learned to tap the sources of strength. It lay also in his refusal to stop with the sensory base of Locke's psychology. The fact that Emerson set out to "transcend" the Lockean premise has blinded many readers to his acceptance of that premise. The essay, it is true, cannot be wholly consistent; it was Emerson's first attempt to move from pulpit to lecture platform, and he wavered between logic and tempting analogies. Yet the Lockean progression is assumed: sensory data as the base, moving by repetition from experience to habit; habit bringing the more abstract concept of continuity and comparison with other habit, continuity suggesting order to the mind, order suggesting generalizations on order as a universal principle; and so to the concept of "laws," which are but the generalizations of man upon his experience and observation but which are also synonymous with "ideas." But ideas are something removed from and transcending the purely sensory experience, and so, for Emerson, are all but synonymous with idealism, moral law, the religious sentiment. Yet all of this is open to the average man, for "in all my lectures, I have taught one doctrine, namely, the infinitude of the private man." [9]

Let us glance briefly at this famous essay *Nature*.[10] Beginning with a reminder that we await in America a native poetry and philosophy developed from our own insights, Emerson defines nature as all that is *not me,* including other men and my own body; in short, all that impinges upon my sensory receptors. A general preface then reminds us that no man is devoid of response to nature, and that "in the woods is perpetual youth."

Emerson then takes up his major argument, the "uses of Nature," in the Lockean order. First is Commodity, that is, food, drink, clothing, tools, the obvious material uses of nature, which all men, without exception, understand. Second he puts Beauty, which is basically a sensory satisfaction derived from the perception of natural forms, though a satisfaction slightly beyond the purely material uses of sight, sound, and touch, and therefore productive of reflections of an ideal sort. Third is Language, defined as the use of symbols for natural objects, every word that exists having its origin in some concrete observation of nature or natural objects. All language is

[9] Emerson, *Journal*, April 7, 1840.
[10] Emerson, *Nature, Works*, I, 7–80.

hence "fossilised poetry," leading to the realm of analogy and "correspondences." Fourth, nature disciplines us, teaches us, that is, the limits of what man can and cannot do in the way of practical action, and so, from a "natural" base, gives man all his science, his tools for mathematics, physics, reasoning itself, proceeding from particular experiences to general skills and knowledge. And finally, from these experiences are built our generalizations, our "laws," the ordering of our observations into general statements that sum up our experience in broader terms than can exist in the world of discrete sensory experiences alone and that therefore project us into the world of "ideas." Such generalizations bespeak our confidence in the reliability of nature; for "any distrust of the permanence of laws [i.e., nature's laws] would paralyze the faculties of man." But a law, when in the mind, is an abstraction, an idea, a form of idealism. Thus we learn from nature the whole progress from simple commodity to idea, to law, to idealism, from experience to the power to see ideal truths amid appearances, and natural phenomena as symbols of the eternal foundations of the universe. Emerson has "transcended" the Lockean limitations on "innate ideas" by finding a new way to the same kind of ideas without the necessity to appeal to the old metaphysical assumptions, leading us back to a renewed confidence in the Platonic world of ideas, but determined, as it were, to approach that Platonic realm afresh from a naturalistic start.

We have admittedly pared Emerson's analogies here to the bare bones of the concreteness of his original empirical foundation, from which they rise. If, in his eagerness to reaffirm his belief in moral values, Emerson hastens over the difficulties within his argument, we may now more confidently assert that at least he did not reject the empirical habit of the eighteenth century or of his own countrymen. Indeed, this becomes clearer with later essays.

So in the bolder and more public statements of "The American Scholar" and "Self-Reliance," Emerson expands on his themes of rejection of the traditional past and the search for original values in the individual intuition. After the "Divinity Address," so shocking to his hearers, there is less reliance on the metaphysical language of the pulpit and a larger secularization of his thinking. The American scholar, he argues, must be a new man, one who has learned from nature and from action; one who respects, but is no slave to, the Past; above all, one who is animated by a profound self-trust, against which neglect, ridicule, and poverty (the scholar's lot) will beat in vain. For it is his high calling, his duty, to be the world's eye, the world's mind, showing men facts amid appearances; and for that calling his freedom must be absolute, bound by his own constitution only. This calling the American is historically fitted best to occupy, and perhaps he alone is so fitted, for does he not "begin life upon our shores, inflated by the mountain winds, shined upon by all the stars of God?" Thus "The American Scholar" is to be read on two levels, that of the historical moment for America to awake from its intellectual lethargy and seek to identify itself with something more than machinery, and that of the deeper admonition to the scholar to assess his own native inheritance and exert himself to possess it. Only so, says Emerson, will "a nation of men . . . for the first time exist," because each feels himself uniquely inspired by the divine soul which inspires all men, and each possesses the freedom of the American to follow the highest of callings.

The ringing summons of "Self-Reliance" are too well known to need summary here. They, too, urge us to heed "the voices which we hear in solitude," to know that living, not expiation, is the goal, and to believe that "nothing is at last sacred but the integrity of your own mind." Here Emerson reaches the classic and probably final expression of the American theme of self-reliance. Little more can be asserted about the transference of that popular virtue to the inner man and his total health; and though the faint-hearted may recoil from its boldness, it remains still a stimulus to the artist, the creative thinker, the creative worker, even the "other directed" and the mentally distraught, all of whom must take heart and know that it is imitation that is suicide, and that each must cultivate his own field for whatever yield it is capable of giving.

Emerson was well aware that he unsettled others. "Only so far as they are unsettled is there any hope for them," he wrote. "Nothing is secure but life, transition, the energizing spirit." [11] "Take which you please," he writes of truth and repose, "you can never have both ... He in whom love of truth predominates will keep himself aloof from all moorings.[12] Religion, too, must start afresh from the individual's experience: "From the pasture, from a boat in the pond, from amidst the songs of woodbirds we possibly may," [13] he writes. Show men, he urges the young divinity students, "a ray of divinity ... clean from all vestige of tradition"; [14] and again, in the "Divinity Address" of 1838, "Let me admonish you, first of all, to go alone—to refuse the good models ... and dare to love God without mediator or veil. ... The imitator dooms himself to a hopeless mediocrity." [15] Here is at least an echo of the intensity of a Jonathan Edwards, and an effort to penetrate to the individual experience and the private verification. And that intensity owes less to German Transcendentalism than to the Puritan, now finally and individually apart, yet united by the reflections of solitude with all men.

In "Circles," Emerson confronts his own extremism: "I am only an experimenter. ... I unsettle all things. No facts to me are sacred; none are profane; I simply experiment, an endless seeker with no Past at my back." [16] In true pioneering fashion, the familiar past is deserted for the unmapped horizons ahead.

From one point of view, Emerson's words may seem a kind of shadowboxing, a denial of the fact, for few Americans were more

[11] Emerson, "Circles," *ibid.,* II, 298.
[12] Emerson, "Intellect," *ibid.,* II, 318.
[13] Emerson, "Circles," *ibid.,* II, 292.
[14] Emerson, "Compensation," *ibid.,* II, 91.
[15] Emerson, "Divinity Address," *ibid.,* I, 143.
[16] Emerson, "Circles," *ibid.,* II, 297.

widely read than Emerson in classical and European literature. "Self-Reliance" has, indeed, been called a whistling in the dark. But look again. Emerson's figures of speech are in no sense those of a man in flight nor those of the barricade; they are those of the explorer, the pioneer in exploration in a region open to all who dare its hazards and its solitudes. Nor is Emerson at all the tormented European romantic, rebellious against he knows not what, uttering anguished protests against ennui and despair. What Emerson asserts is the parallel of Thoreau's liberty to play the new American, to build his own rude shelter out of the materials available to him on the frontiers of thought, and there to explore what needs exploring, whatever the risks. Behind that placid exterior of Emerson's is a rugged quality of endurance and self-control in the face of heavy oppositions.

It is no original observation that Emerson's figures of speech are drawn often from the homely, the daily experience. "I embrace the common," he says in "The American Scholar." "I explore and sit at the feet of the familiar, the low. Give me insight into today and you may have the antique and future worlds. What would we really know the meaning of? The meal in the firkin; the milk in the pan; the ballad in the street." [17] His similes remain those of the New England village; and behind the apparent Platonism is a shrewd New England villager's eye, a Yankee observation, that did not always spare neighbors and their daily living. His impulses were democratic, in which he differed from his friend Carlyle. "Let us treat men and women well;" he wrote; "treat them as if they were real; perhaps they are." [18]

Nevertheless, the voice of Emerson is finally that of the cultivated New Englander; he is no mud-on-the-boots frontiersman, and much that he said smells of the library and the packed notebooks. He excused his bookishness, his acquaintance with many authors, by

[17] Emerson, "The American Scholar," *ibid.,* I, 110.
[18] Emerson, "Experience," *ibid.,* III, 63.

his theory of books: that they were but the stimulation of the scholar's idle moments, not his true task. Great writers, he reminded his audience, were themselves once young men in libraries; and great nations, he might have added, had once the independence of youth. Yet he was in part the victim of his own library; and his tags from Montaigne, Swedenborg, the neo-Platonist English poets, the Oriental mystics, kept getting in his way or pulling him back to his innate impulse to be an admonisher and ethical leader. His was hardly the new language of the raw west.

Emerson was not, at his best, a derivative thinker, and it was his hope and aim to escape such a charge. He would submit all to his own thinking, for only so could he create that which was original, native, authentic, true to self. All else must be thrust aside when his central mission called. Like his follower Whitman, he must hold

> Creeds and schools in abeyance,
> Retiring back a while sufficed at what they are . . .
> I harbor for good or bad, I permit to speak at every hazard,
> Nature without check with original energy.[19]

The risk, obviously, was thinness, scholarly superficiality, over-emphasis on rejection, bravado in the face of history's long and informative tale, even a misguided confidence in one's own insights. Yet try it he must, and try it we, as Americans, must. Emerson's instinct was true.

Somehow it eluded him—this American certainty. It seemed always almost within reach. One more essay, one more dredging of self and the notebooks, one more confident assertion of the rightness of self-trust, and all would be clear. "Long must he stammer," he had said early in his career; and he accepted the handicap, assured of the reward in the end. So he explored Nature first—all must be from the original experience, within the known, solid, direct, reliable, sensory, within the initial reach of all. But he had also to find his

---

[19] Whitman, *Song of Myself*, Stanza 1, *Complete Poetry*.

way somehow to idealism, for his was still the Puritan conscience and the clerical habit. He capped nature with more and more nebulous "correspondences" and abstractions, eked out with quotations from George Herbert, Plotinus, and "a certain poet," a compound of his envisioned self and his friend Bronson Alcott.

It eluded him still. He tried again in "The American Scholar," a more secular and a popular subject, declaring in his address the native independence, the inherent self-confidence of his nation, the goodly prospects. Encouraged, he admonished the young ministers the next year to trust the inner oracle; and he launched then on "Self-Reliance," asserting in valiant phrases the genius of self-trust, the folly of imitation, the madness of conformity, the rewards that await the bold and the confident. It was a masterly clearing of the ground for action, and he felt stripped for great things. But he had not arrived yet at what he wanted to say. There were flashes of it, gleams within the subsequent essays, encouragements to others. But there were always the compromises to be made with life as it is— the need for tolerance toward all, for sympathy with the seekers, the recognition of tensions that came with fame and reputation, the demands for ethical leadership. And there were the harder shocks, the early death of his wife and of his four-year-old son, the loss of his home by fire, the tragedy of his brothers. "Nature is what you may do. There is much you may not," he had to admit in his essay "Fate." [20] Those who think Emerson knew nothing of the harsher sides of reality or sought a monkish escape from such realities should read thoughtfully "Experience" and "Fate," and again "Illusion." Like his countrymen, Emerson learned the nature of conflict and felt the shadows of the war between North and South. Nevertheless, he remained a primary voice on the frontiers of thought, and many were indebted to him and his liberating energies.

Even less than Emerson did Thoreau dwell worshipfully in the

[20] Emerson, "Fate," *Works,* VI, 20.

past. Likewise a reader, his very love of the ancient Greek classics
arose from their freshness in the story of the human mind, and
books were for him even less of a necessity for the expression of
himself. Who has sung more eloquently the enchantments of nature
and solitude, the individual man's quiet joy in the presence of an
uncrowded skyline? It is unimportant that Thoreau's withdrawal
from society was but temporary and partial; he went not to flee, but
to explore his own resources. The economics of that withdrawal, too,
was exploratory. He faced the problem that every creative artist
knows; for poems, symphonies, or scientific discoveries are not composed in the busy market place, and one without money must
either resign his urge to create while he earns a livelihood, or
learn how to live with a minimum of necessities. That minimum
of living, however, is no guarantee of the greatness of the creative
product; and this, too, Thoreau, as Emerson, knew. The exploration went deeper than economics. Thoreau became a one-man laboratory of research into the minimal cost of survival in an acquisitive
society, and into the complex chemistry and biology of the creative
act.

Thoreau sought the rejuvenation of men's powers, of his innocence in the face of nature—"in the wind and rain which never
die." [21] Again and again his phrases have about them this flash of
the magic of a natural simplicity. He lives as an author because of
this hard-earned gift, a gift earned by shedding the rhetoric of the
classroom, by soaking himself in the simple experience of living in
nature, by weighing each phrase for its hard core of reality. He must
combine the hardness, the physical vitality, of the frontiersman with
the reflections of a civilized man. Like Cooper's Natty Bumppo, he
would represent the innocence of each without the vices of either.
And if the frontier tested a man's resolution, the universe was a
vastly larger testing ground. Self-denial was less a virtue, an end,

[21] Thoreau, *A Week, Writings,* I, 8.

than it was the training of the athlete for a performance far beyond the ordinary, an exhibition of what a man could aim at.

More rigorously, more concretely than Emerson, Thoreau sought always the basic reality. Listen to him:

> Let us settle ourselves, and work and wedge our feet downward through the mud and slush of opinion, and prejudice, and tradition, and delusion, and appearance, that alluvion which covers the globe, through Paris and London, through New York and Boston and Concord, through church and state, through poetry and philosophy and religion, till we come to a hard bottom and rocks in place, which we can call *reality*, and say, This is, and no mistake; and then begin, having a *point d'appui*, below freshet and frost and fire, a place where you might found a wall or a state. . . . Be it life or death, we crave only reality.[22]

These are strong and moving words, and behind them must be a long immersion in independency of mind and geography. It is only fair to ask how Thoreau would accomplish this tremendous plunge toward reality. His answer will always be in terms of the individual and the individual in close contact with nature. Man had once worked his way up from the unvarnished realities of nature, living as animals and savages know how to live; to nature he must return often and often for the factual base and for insight. "Nature," says Henry Thoreau, "puts no questions and answers none which we mortals ask. She has long ago taken her resolution." [23] Here, too, is the Puritan's grim satisfaction in that which is set and predestined, leaving him only the choice of acceptance or rejection, though Thoreau's tone is lightened by a wry, Yankee irony in the contemplation of things. The forces of nature take their time, and men, in the meantime, live partial rather than doomed lives.

"It would be some advantage," he writes at the outset of *Walden*, "to live a primitive and frontier life, though in the midst of an

---

[22] Thoreau, *Walden, ibid.*, II, 154.
[23] *Ibid.*, 436.

outward civilization, if only to learn what are the gross necessaries of life and what methods have been taken to obtain them." [24] The same reflection applies to the deeper issues of life. Thoreau went to Walden Pond, as he explained, to front the essential facts of living, "and not, when I came to die, discover that I had not lived." The basic rule for the experiment, local or cosmic, must be always simplicity, simplicity, and again simplicity, and the "perpetual instilling and drenching of the reality that surrounds us." [25]

Thoreau's subject was nature, almost to specialization; but it was, even more, human nature, which he could never divorce from man's natural setting. "Let us spend one day as deliberately as Nature," he urges, just before the famous passage above on reality; and his conclusion to *Walden* is entirely a reiteration of the frontier metaphor, applied in detail to the way a man should live: "Be . . . the Lewis and Clark . . . of your own streams and oceans; explore your own higher latitudes. . . . Be a Columbus to whole new continents . . . of thought. . . . Explore thyself. Herein are demanded the eye and the nerve . . . Start now on that farthest western way." [26]

Obviously, Thoreau was no dry literalist of nature, but a poet and a philosopher, and, in the antique Stoic mold, a rebuker of his fellow men in the bargain. The persistent didacticism of his pages sometimes betrays him into lapses beneath his best intentions. Yet Thoreau had a more practical eye than Emerson, and nothing of the pulpit. He knew the use of common tools; and he observed with the farmer's calculation that man did not survive and find food unless he worked with the seasons. This whole new continent, he clearly foresaw, lay not for conquest as an enemy, but for consideration, as an ally. Man might survive on it forever, feeling its might and its gifts beneath him, but not by warfare upon it; the price was understanding of nature's ways, the nice balance between man's

[24] *Ibid.*, 21.
[25] *Ibid.*, 153.
[26] *Ibid.*, 495–497 *passim*.

needs and nature's storehouse, and the replenishment of that store-house in a sympathetic partnership. Machines, he concluded long before politicians could be aroused to the meaning of conservation, return nothing to nature, neither seed nor fertilization; and animals and birds once extinct, minerals and ores and chemicals once vanished, never return. Man and nature, man in nature, this was the inescapable duality, nay, unity, the true health, the inescapable union. "Your scheme," he wrote, "must be the framework of the universe; all other schemes will soon be ruins." [27]

Thus Thoreau's solitary excursions were made in search of the secrets of nature, the lore of Indians and how they survived, the study of men and farms and valleys and woods. He was made of the stuff that might readily have walked to Canada and back, to Oregon, if need be. He had no fear of nights alone without shelter, or days of solitary contemplation on the ways of birds and fish and slumbering lakes. He said once, Emerson recalled, to one who offered to accompany him on a walk, that he "had no walks to throw away on company." [28] Even less could he abide interference with a man's right to his own constitution. "If I knew for a certainty," he says in *Walden,* "that a man was coming to my house with the conscious design of doing me good, I should run for my life." [29] "I would have each one," he says again in *Walden,* "be very careful to find out and pursue *his own* way, and not his father's or his mother's or his neighbor's." [30] Looking abroad at his own society, and thinking of slavery, he complains: "Wherever a man goes, men will pursue and paw him with their dirty institutions." Such was the animus of his essay on "Civil Disobedience." It was not that he wanted no government, but at once a better one than that which condoned the literal enslavement of six million human beings; until that was cor-

[27] Thoreau, *A Week, Writings,* I, 88.
[28] Emerson, "Thoreau," *Works,* X, 434.
[29] Thoreau, *Walden, Writings,* II, 118.
[30] *Ibid.,* 113.

rected, he could not subscribe to the state. He might, he added, "have run 'amok' against society; but I preferred that society should run 'amok' against me, it being the desperate party." [31]

Thoreau's was an individualism such as had seldom been seen, such as may perhaps never be seen again. There was both humor and local color in his one-man defiance of society. True, it was not difficult to speak so boldly in the Concord of the 1840's, as it was not difficult to be bold in defiance of old restraints on the frontier. The humor in Thoreau is made possible by the free and open society in which he lived. His outspoken phrases can provoke us not only to personal revaluations; they can suggest that a Thoreau is a measure of how free a society is or can be. That State which can afford a Thoreau is free. In our own sadder century, a few brave individuals have had once again the opportunity to test their fortitude, to rise above their States, but at a price which underlines our decay and the danger of our return to all that which we once politically renounced.

[31] *Ibid.*, 268.

ix. The Cost of Solitude

SOLITUDE must exact its price as well as promise its rewards; and it was this other side of the coin that Hawthorne and Melville (not to mention Poe) tested. In vain the Transcendentalists sang the virtues of self-reliance and a benign and silent communion with nature. A heavy restraint, a deep inner self-distrust and suspicion of man's nature, hung like a veil over these descendants of the Puritans, and made difficult all their efforts at escape. Their maturity came slowly; they had not the outlet of the active frontier but the habits of self-denial. Their enemy was dual: the pessimism inherent in Calvinism, and the communal suspicion that all arts were a kind of frivolity beneath grown men. One had to be an outsider, like Whitman, to take the world as an open road.

Emerson occasionally recognized the limitations of solitude. "Nature," he said in his essay "Fate," "is no sentimentalist";[1] and to his *Journal* he confided, after a conversation with Thoreau, "We stated over again, to sadness almost, the eternal loneliness. . . . How insular

[1] Emerson, "Fate," *Works*, VI, 12.

and sadly pathetically solitary are all the people we know." [2] In that loneliness the high-sounding phrases sometimes vibrated thinly, lacking the warmth of living action.

No one knew the secrets of loneliness more inwardly than Nathaniel Hawthorne. His central theme came almost to be summed up in one word, *solitude*—solitude as a curse, a punishment, an icy hand laid upon the heart, the dark shadows of the New England forests penetrating the very walls of old houses. Hawthorne might almost have been consciously exploring De Tocqueville's sharp observation that individualism in America throws every man "back forever upon himself alone and threatens in the end to confine him entirely within the solitude of his own heart." [3] But Hawthorne had no need to quote others. His knowledge, like that of his countrymen, was self-experienced, self-tested, and inward.

In considering the genesis of a talent like Hawthorne's, the most New England of our major writers, the truest of guides to the inner recesses of the Puritan as inheritance had marked him, we must look far less to the frontier spirit as we have characterized it than to the old New England of witchcraft, King Philip's War, the sermons of the Mathers and of Jonathan Edwards, and the lingering remnants of that past even into the great days of New England shipping and industry. Rather than dwell on the many biographies of this introverted man, let us consider for a moment a penetrating essay by Allen Tate on another New England figure, Emily Dickinson, equally New England, more local than Hawthorne, equally knowledgeable in the ways of solitude, even less identifiable as to teacher or source. Says Tate, in explanation of this phenomenon of an artist of power from an environment which would seem unfruitful, "It is the effort of the individual to live apart from a cultural tradition that no longer sustains him." But this tradition

[2] Emerson's *Journal*, October 27, 1851. The sentence "How insular . . ." was repeated in "Society and Solitude," *Works*, VII, 15.
[3] De Tocqueville, *Democracy in America*, II, 106.

must still be a force, powerful enough to set up the tensions of the creative mind; for "poetry does not dispense with tradition; it probes the deficiencies of a tradition."[4]

Here, it would seem, is precisely the dilemma of Hawthorne. The old Puritan tradition is for him no longer viable; yet it is still a force to be reckoned with. Hence he must probe its power, its deficiencies, must get it in perspective, must seek some resolution. Emerson's bland eclecticism and confidence are not for him, nor is Thoreau's log-cabin retreat. Yet he is far too much a son of the native dissidence to dwell in any Old World answer. His skepticism is neither perverse nor shallowly mean, but stems from a deep loyalty to his own vision and knowledge, a kind of self-reliance which in its solitary way is as independent as anything Emerson proposed and far more withdrawn from dependence on others than was Thoreau's cabin.

Such a temperament, Mr. Tate suggests, is not on the level of the intellectually conscious alone; and this explains how he can say of Emily Dickinson that, though she is a great poet, "She cannot reason at all. She can only *see*."[5] So one might conclude of Hawthorne that though he was an analyst of human psychology, he was no philosopher. Whence, then, the power of this kind of writer? Tate, making use of further examples, such as John Donne and Shakespeare, suggests three component elements:

1) All is "put to the concrete test of experience . . . We are not told what to think; we are told to look at the situation."[6]

2) The ideas are the writer's own, neither borrowed nor quoted, but an expression of the very centers of the writer's being.

3) The writer has accepted no ready-made nor pat solution, has not even listened to his or her own private preference or desire.

---

[4] Allen Tate, "Emily Dickinson," *Collected Essays*, p. 208.
[5] *Ibid.*, p. 205.
[6] *Ibid.*, p. 206.

The thing is seen as a problem to be set forth with clarity, not as a campaign to convert.

In short, Emily Dickinson (and so, too, our Hawthorne) "speaks wholly to the individual experience." [7] The literary expression, in both cases, emerges from private tensions embedded deeply within the writer's individual character and inheritance.

We have dwelt for a moment on Mr. Tate's reasoning because it is pertinent not only to Emily Dickinson and to Hawthorne but to our whole theme of the American's habit of direct reference to experience. Being novelist and story teller, as Emerson and Thoreau were not, Hawthorne cast his dilemmas into fictional and concrete terms as experiences knowable by actual human beings. Such, indeed, is the nature of all good fiction at its best, and Tate's criteria have a much wider application than to the single writers under discussion.

Hawthorne has more than once been characterized as the skeptic, the one who does not find it possible to propose the ready-made solution for what are individual dilemmas. The tensions, the conflicts, of his stories are all inward, on the battlefields of secret guilt and personal isolation. They have consequences rather than solutions, with the result that Hawthorne's themes are often put in the form of a question. Hawthorne had neither the hard Puritan certitudes—the Puritan flaw, if you will—of harsh judgment on others, nor any other such simple scale by which to estimate the immediate guilt or innocence of each situation. Hence he is able to examine the elements of his problem in a fashion that foreshadows a more modern psychological interest, referring each to its own setting, its own outcome in the individual character. Hawthorne lets us see the Puritan conscience at work, even while he introduces the element of questioning its harsh determinism. It is as if he said, not that the Puritan view is true, but what happens if you act and live as if it were true?

[7] *Ibid.*, p. 213.

Ancient wrongs, ancient cruelties, shadowy deeds known only to their perpetrators but bringing their inevitable consequences just the same, sins made such by the Puritan rigidity which knows no gradations between righteousness and evil, eccentricities born of isolation and delusion—such are the themes for Hawthorne's brooding contemplation. And since the settings are most often those of a New England past, in the background loom the deep, dark New England forests, lonely paths beneath the arching branches, the dim recesses of old houses, the dwellings of those who have somehow stepped aside from the main currents of life. The end is tragedy, none the less so if often of a low and lingering intensity, the tragedy of wasted lives and unnecessary denials. The escape, if any, is found only by merging once more into the human stream, with all its imperfections, and by denying or withholding acquiescence to the Puritan will.

In his quiet, self-effacing way, Hawthorne is as remote from communal commitments, as indifferent to conventions, as the most radical of Transcendentalists, as the farthest of frontiersmen. But his individualism is less romantic, nearer that of Emily Dickinson's "gallanter," who "charge within the bosom the Cavalry of Wo." Hawthorne in his own setting is as American as any. Not only does he place nearly all of his stories up to his later work in New England settings; his themes are those suggested by the New England past as under the burden of the wilderness it shifted from the original drive to its high quota of introversion and ingrown consciences and individuals left behind in the bustling westward movement of a growing nation. Hawthorne has as little interest as has Thoreau in political forms, police regulations, social conformities, and churchly conventions. His dilemmas are never social, always individual; the psychology of the isolated become eccentric in the withdrawn circle of self. His landscapes are inevitably those of the lonely forest, the shadowy interior of old houses, the solitary meditation.

Hawthorne would seem to have launched his tales while still held by a kind of determinism. In one of his earliest tales, "Wakefield," a man steps aside from the normal habits of family life with increasing frequency, impelled by a strange perversity toward isolation, and, when close to insanity, discovers that "an influence beyond our control lays its strong hand on every deed which we do, and weaves its consequences into an iron tissue of necessity." [8] This, along with its corollary observation that once a man steps aside he cannot find his place in the procession again, forms a grim motto for any tale. Its implications hang over many of Hawthorne's stories: "Roger Malvin's Burial," "The Ambitious Guest," "The White Old Maid," "Young Goodman Brown," "The Maypole of Merry Mount." In one form or another, the inevitability of "influences beyond our control" may be detected. Yet such cannot be the final statement on Hawthorne; for increasingly his stories leave open the query: might it be, might it have been, something else? Finally, late in his work, in *The Marble Faun*, he arrives, though in the tentative words of Kenyon, half afraid of his own boldness, to an open doubt more nearly conformable to American optimism: is it possible that sin, like sorrow, is an educative factor in our progress toward goals we might not otherwise have attained?

How often the forest returns in Hawthorne as an integral part of his tale, the vast forest that shadowed the whole eastern coast, broken only by the cleared spaces, the streams that served as colonial highways, and the lakes that lay hidden in their depths. Even the savages that lurked in these shades, Thoreau remarked, may come themselves to have been dreamed up, as if "our bold ancestors . . . were not struggling rather with the forest shadows . . . vapors, fever and ague of the unsettled woods." [9] For Hawthorne that forest is the symbol of the dark heart of man, the untamed member which

---

[8] References are to Hawthorne's *Complete Works*.
[9] Thoreau, *A Week, Writings*, I, 219.

refuses subjugation to the inherited law. The frontiersman's boast
has become the moralist's dilemma; and Hawthorne, before Melville, removes from a rising American literature the charge of a
naive optimism.

In "The Maypole of Merry Mount," in a primitive forest setting,
a little clearing surrounded by the dusky woods, where "jollity and
gloom were contending for an empire," a local incident of no great
import spreads to a universal observation. Premature, at least,
seemed the jollity in the face of the vast labors ahead before one
might view an empire of homes and civilized manners. The gloom
is double, that of the endless, looming forest, and that of the Puritans who emerge like shadows to rebuke and end the merriment.
For soon "the shadows of the forest mingle gloomily in the dance";
and finally the followers of the stern Endicott peremptorily end
the jollity and enforce the theme: "As the moral gloom of the
world overpowers all systematic gaity, even so was their home of
wild mirth made desolate amid the sad forest." The Puritans are
not the voice of the forest; quite the contrary, they are the reminder
that life is serious so long as the dark forests and caverns of human
guilt remain untamed.

Again, in "Roger Malvin's Burial," how unforgettable is the
native setting for both beginning and end, the wounded older man
and the youth completely alone in the depths of the woods, the
frontier of 1725, following a battle with the Indians; the older man
urging the younger to abandon him, for "wherefore should I not
rest beneath the open sky, covered only by the oak leaves when the
autumn wind shall strew them?" Yet the dying man extracts the
promise of the youth's return, inaugurating thereby the secret guilt
of a broken promise and, many years later, the terrible retribution in
the selfsame forest setting by means of the—was it accidental?—
shooting of the youth's own son, the old man's grandson. Here the
Puritan past and the New England frontier are blended in a lonely
and moving tale.

In "Young Goodman Brown," another young man steps into a dark forest and there encounters the Puritan theme of total depravity in the person of his neighbors, his own wife, Faith, and himself, and in consequence of this revelation remains forever a sad and melancholy man. Yet it is the Satanic leader of the forest revels who points this moral and who invites young Goodman into the universal communion. Has Hawthorne, then, approved or scrutinized the Puritan belief? Perhaps it was only a dream, he says; it was, nevertheless, a dream of bad omen for the young man. These dreams in Hawthorne's tales are not passing ones merely; they are often the hidden fears of the solitary, the withdrawn, those committed to a point of view which denies the common human brotherhood, those wrestling with the age-old problems of humanity in the isolation of the private soul.

But Hawthorne could not linger here, and a kind of moral democracy begins to invade his tales. The unpardonable sin, in the end, is to cut oneself off from the common stream; and the dread punishment is isolation from one's fellowmen. "Man must not disclaim his brotherhood, even with the guiltiest," he concludes, "since, though his hand be clean, his heart has surely been polluted by the flitting phantoms of iniquity." [10] The broader claims of humanity take precedence finally over the narrower gloom and special "election" of the Puritan, and Hawthorne is still redeemable for the more native party of hope. Nor have his individuals, whatever their sufferings, renounced the American habit of self-reference. But the price is heavy, and the vaunted blessings of solitude are tinged with a somber hue.

The Scarlet Letter is uniformly recognized as Hawthorne's masterpiece. We shall not pause here to dwell on the obvious, the tiny frontier village set within the untamed forests, and the intricate symbolism throughout. This has been well explored in more than

[10] Hawthorne, "Fancy's Show Box," *Complete Works*, I, 257.

one study. How powerfully here are frontier setting and individual
isolation interwoven, despite the presence of a closely knit theocratic
society. Yet even in this stern community, where the central figure,
Dimmesdale, is both clergyman and sinner, both judge and condemned, the punishment is in no slightest degree that of either
court or church, but is within the secret cell of his own being; for
Dimmesdale has forfeited his link with the common humanity by
denying, not his deed, which is human, but love, paternity, the
human bond that might have saved him. Hester, the branded one,
is the one character of dignity and nobility in the book, beside whom
the villagers are a mean and petty lot of gossipers. She is likewise
the embodiment of self-reliance, for there is for her no law save that
of love. She hides nothing but the name of her lover, and even that
is done out of pity and protection for the weaker one. The truly
evil character is the wronged husband, the Old World scientist,
who wronged his wife in the beginning by a loveless marriage, and
who wronged the frail Dimmesdale far more than the clergyman
had wronged him.

Hawthorne's little classic is quite misconceived if it is read as a
tale with a conventional moral of sin punished. Indeed, the book
fully meets Allen Tate's criteria for a literature of tensions: it probes
a culture for its deficiencies, it is not satisfied with a conventional
answer, it remains objective. The conflict is between the thinness,
the insufficiency, of the Puritan ideal as embodied in the ascetic
Dimmesdale, and the human warmth of a common bond in love and
the child. If Goodman Brown found that common bond to be one
of horror and evil, as Calvin had taught, Dimmesdale no less sacrificed himself on that same altar of Puritan logic, renouncing the
closest of human ties for what might, after all, have been also a
dream. The isolation, it is true, is that of a Puritan soul, but the
forest setting gives it a frame that no settled land could have
equalled. The Puritan incompleteness is paralleled by the cultural
meagerness of a society cut off from the larger stream, within

which isolation can intensify the inner struggle of each individual. Even that ambiguous tale, "Rapaccini's Daughter," carries, it is probable, a meaning not too dissimilar. Giovanni, indeed, is a Puritan finding evil in Beatrice's more normal desire for human warmth and sympathy; and her final cry is, "Oh, was there not, from the first, more poison in thy nature than in mine?" In final analysis, Hawthorne, deeply Puritan, deeply New England, feels his way back to the inheritance of an experiment in separation, geographical as well as communal, tests the consequences of both, and like the others gropes his way toward the newer party of hope and the newer western man. In New England, rejection of the past was less simple than on the western frontiers.

And what of nature and solitude in Herman Melville? Melville's books are filled with the variety and bustle of American life and character, not only of the open sea but also of seaport and inland life. He touches also Mississippi traffic and the Berkshire hills, and, in *Pierre,* the rural landscape of upper New York state, the city-scapes of Albany and New York. He was as truly indigenous as any American author, and in his bones felt the past, the great western levels, and the call of the sea. He accepted, too, the legend of a special mission for America. "We are the pioneers of the world," he affirms in *White-Jacket,* "the advance guard, sent on through the wilderness of untried things, to break a new path in the New World that is ours." [11] To this jaunty confidence are joined the familiar tones of rejection of the past, the "lumbering baggage-wagons of old Precedents." In *Israel Potter,* describing his heroic figure, Ethan Allen, he writes, "His spirit was essentially Western; and herein is his peculiar Americanism; for the Western spirit is, or will yet be (for no other is, or can be), the true American one." [12] The tale of Captain Ahab, quite apart from its wealth of symbol-

[11] Herman Melville, *White-Jacket,* pp. 142–143.
[12] Melville, *Israel Potter,* p. 241. Bulkington appears in *Moby-Dick,* Chapter XXIII.

ism, and taken as a literal story, might well have been that of an American folk hero, paralleling on sea the exploits of Daniel Boone or Davy Crockett on land. Read simply as a record of the growth of the American whaling industry (whose vessels outnumbered those of the rest of the world), *Moby-Dick* might have been, and perhaps was originally planned to be, as much the embodiment of the American boast as any tale of the far west. It contains the same ingredients of heroic deeds against great natural odds, endurance, hardihood, competence in the struggle with nature and her wilder forms, the frontiersman's individual wit and skill pitted on the grand scale against all obstacles. But Melville, presumably fired by his discovery of Hawthorne's "great power of blackness," chose to magnify his hero into almost superhuman proportions, and to make of him an obsessive exploration of the whole metaphor of self-reliance on the frontiers of thought and experience.

Herein lies the difference. Melville no less than Emerson admired the independence of the self-reliant individual. His Bulkington has been mentioned before: "All deep, earnest thinking is but the intrepid effort of the soul to keep the open independence of her sea . . . In landlessness alone resides the highest truth." Melville in person had seen the other face of nature, the face of danger and hardship and solitude in her vast, impassive embrace; he could never rest in a bland optimism. His months among the savages of Tahiti had exposed him to the attractions of the primitive but no less to the cannibalism, actual and figurative, that accompanied primitivism. Like the first western explorers, he had been thrown early into a tough world, among savages and among those of his own race no less savage. "Your true whale-hunter," he observes in *Moby-Dick,* "is as much a savage as an Iroquois." Such experiences did not encourage a purely romantic view of nature, nor did solitude seem wholly designed to be inspirational. Ishmael, in a reverie induced by a calm on the ocean, reflects that beneath that calm and peacefulness lie the teeming horrors of sharks and the deep drowning that awaits the single miscalculation. "Heed it well, ye Pantheists!" he ejaculates.

Captain Ahab, like Emerson, may be seen as a spare Yankee idealist, but with what a difference. For to Ahab there is malignancy behind that deceptive calm, a hidden power that shows itself in the very casualness of its storms and furies, a cruelty in the Arctic wastes and the prairie snows, sufficient to frighten the very will of man to survive.

Let us devise a little scene. The slender, scholarly Emerson stands upon a platform before an audience of polite cultivation, uttering his smoothly rounded sentences of inspiration, extolling nature as symbol of spirit, man's deepest intuitions as reliable revelations, solitude as a source of virtue and idealism. Suddenly there appears beside him a gaunt figure, equally slender, equally tall, equally spare, equally New England in visage and speech, but how much grimmer—Captain Ahab. Consider well that tanned and seamed countenance, that grim visage, accustomed to command in situations of direst danger, that wooden leg replacing the one bit off by the hugest of nature's gentle creations, that unexplained scar that runs down face and neck and apparently the whole body, as if the lightnings of nature's benign intention had streaked the living man, that cold, blue eye that has outstared Atlantic and Pacific gales, that taciturn jaw that bespeaks the unyielding will. Behind that firm brow lie the memories of months and years of solitude on uncharted seas and of long, lost voyages in search of the very limits of nature's meaning. That knowledge of death and danger in small frail tubs of wood, and of men plunged into icy waters infested with sharks, is direct and personal. For Captain Ahab is real enough, and in his actual experience and knowledge no mere figment of the imagination. Shall we invite this man for a quiet stroll in the New England fields and woods, where he may analogize Nature and the correspondences with the Over-Soul?

Obviously, Melville's vision is quite otherwise. It is neither Hawthorne's brooding withdrawal nor Thoreau's excursions around a small pond, for Melville is a tempestuous man, by temperament a fighter. And his Ahab, for all his brooding intensity, is no less a competent American, a frontiersman of a new sort. He is wholly native, a hunter, an explorer, a wanderer, a doer, an individualist, a capitalist, a seeker. His spirit is that which crosses continents, dares unknown horizons, savages, and wild beasts, challenges what lies beyond the most distant sky. He is, in short, a master of self-reliance and the resolute will.

What is nature to this man? After long knowledge, suffering, and brooding upon experience that has taken him around the globe itself, he has come to see nature as a noncommunicative mask, concealing a blind, indifferent, possibly even a malevolent force, or, worse still, no power at all, but a sheer, mechanical, conscienceless force. What, then, shall a man do? Being Ahab, Ahab will pit against nature his indomitable will and all his frontiersman's wit and skill. In his obsessed mind, the whale, hugest, most powerful, and most elusive of all of nature's active symbols, is the living representation of that cosmic riddle. If nature be man's enemy, resolute man can but resist, with all that he has. And if the whale be nature's chief emissary, against the whale must Ahab voyage, until he force from it and nature the admission of man's will and superiority. If, however, nature be naught but mechanical force, and man alone in it be brain, soul, will, must he not even more assert himself against nature's mindless monsters, pitting mind against mindlessness?

Is Ahab mad? We can only answer yes and no. On the practical side, he is wholly himself, a first-class captain, and none better. He makes no mistakes as a whaler; he is respected and feared by his crew; he knows the oceans as Mark Twain knew the Mississippi and Jim Bridger the western mountains. He is competent to the point of legend. His madness is not in his competence but in his obsession that the final test of his ability will be to capture that one elusive whale. Even here, on the simple, factual side, he may be but one more good man who wishes to prove that he can be champion, can climb Everest, or drive the fastest car, or encircle the globe in a capsule. But there is more: he will also assert in the doing what it is to be man in the face of an indifferent nature, man on the very frontiers of human achievement, man alone and barehanded where he must rely on himself. The metaphysical involvement comes on top of this human reality, not outside of it.

How foolish, again, to read a conventional moral into a great piece of fiction. Ahab can be no simple allegory of good and evil; when Melville wrote Hawthorne that *Moby-Dick* was "a wicked book," he knew well that such a book could never rest in the conventional patterns. The whale can never be simply evil (that vague abstraction) to be overcome, for that would make Ahab a passionate reformer. The whale is not supernatural; it does nothing that a whale might not do, has not done; caught, it would have yielded whale oil like the rest, and today would succumb easily to unromantic weapons which treat the whale as beneath respect. Ahab, as man and as sea captain, is not superhuman, though immensely competent. What he is is another American seeker, who, in Emersonian terms, has discarded the past and confronts experience directly, head on, without intermediary—who, in De Tocqueville's phrase, must "strike through the mask to substance." However strange his obsession, what he confronts is not merely fictional, but is close to the very mystery of existence. Though his conclusions be different from those of Emerson or Edwards, his practical knowledge and experience have been vastly greater, on the very frontiers of human endurance and testing, and for his evidence he draws on bitterness and defeat and long hours of confinement in his lonely cabin on the sea.

How could he, then, be Good against Evil, a simple morality-play confrontation; or how could he be Satan, when he openly complains of his human infirmities, physical and mental? No, he is Man tortured by a too-near gaze into the solitary experience, as Emerson's Scholar is Man Thinking in his study, but for the world. Melville makes it clear enough: "All that most maddens and torments . . . all truth with malice in it; all that cracks the sinews and cakes the brain; all the subtle demonisms of life and thought," these Ahab piled upon the white whale's hump and "burst his hot heart's shell upon it." [13] With a reliance on self so deep as to be obsessive, with a desire to know with an immediacy that is almost insanity, Ahab is a kind of Yankee mystic in reverse.

Ahab is thus within the American pattern of the student of nature and solitude, even though it lead him to suspect that behind the mask of beauty and storm, nature's "invisible spheres were formed in fright." A true romantic in this, that he has staked all on his passionate compulsion, his impulse is not to trust but to mistrust nature's silent message. Like Emerson, he cannot avoid the metaphysical that lies hidden behind the obvious and the concrete; like Emerson, he cannot find the old answers satisfactory. Unlike Emerson, and perhaps thereby more American, he will not turn aside from the harshest of frontiers, the one on which the horizon lies forever beyond.

Are American whales so far to seek? John Brown's whale was slavery and the United States government, alike huge and palpable symbols of all that obstructed justice within the American promise. Like Ahab, John Brown must pit a solitary self against the whale, and lose to a rope around his neck. Thoreau's whale was encroaching society, the state, the machine, all mechanical devourers of man as individual. The Puritan's whale was man's proneness to evil, which he labelled "total depravity," and against which he staked a new Zion. He lost to practical necessities and the stubbornness of human nature. Hawthorne's whale was this same Puritan inheritance, demanding total submission to its hard denial of

[13] Melville, *Moby-Dick*, Chapter XLI.

the human will, against which Hawthorne could only suggest that man, like Ahab, might be the victim of a bad dream. Woodrow Wilson's whale was international wars, against which he threw the American hope of an innate better judgment in man under reason, and his own enfeebled strength, only to end in apparent defeat.

Like Ahab, these men must assault the whale in person, and not, like common humanity, leave all for time and human convention to defer in endless evasion. Each such figure, in the name of an abstraction, refuses to deny the Utopian goal that experience has shown to be unattainable, and renews the effort and the challenge. The curious thing is that though the past, from its long experience, has taught submission and conformity, the open frontiers of land and sea appear to engender a refusal to accept that answer as final. On the one hand has been the ambition of human power to organize and to compel; on the other, the lonely resistance of the individual, doomed to defeat, but resistant still. To call this compulsion metaphysical is not wholly inexact. The whale itself is merely another terrestrial creature, within the general pattern. But beyond it are the unanswering spheres. Behind the concrete statistics of nuclear power and reproductive explosion, behind the ruthless threats of political might and the knowledge of human cruelty, the face is the face of nature, the enigma is Ahab's own: why man, the solitary individual, must seek to penetrate the mask. Our new seas are the infinite spaces, where swim the planets and the stars. What whales man may there encounter, we cannot know; but be assured he will not hesitate for that.

x. The Poet Comes

THE FRONTIERS of the New World, land and water, as first-hand experience with nature and its many solitudes, found expression again and again in American writers, whether in patriotic self-congratulation at the widening challenge, the sense of a new freedom and a new felicity, or in the exploration of what might be done with new idioms, new materials, and new metaphors. On the one hand, the story of the expanding frontier had suggested a corollary in a new kind of man and the possibility of a native idealism unhampered by the old past and fortified by individual insights; on the other, the price of the individual's withdrawal from other human beings, the darker knowledge of loneliness and terror, had touched the new literature with a somber note, the suspicion of enigmas not to be solved so easily by independence and rejection of the past.

Still the dream of a powerful native voice persisted, one speaking for the American experience, without indebtedness to the old models. Was this hope to be doomed to failure? In 1844 Emerson put the hope and the sense of delay:

We have yet had no genius in America . . . [who] knew the value of our incomparable materials. . . . Our logrolling, our stumps and their politics, our fisheries, our Negroes, and Indians, our boats, and our re-pudiations . . . the northern trade, the southern planting, the western clearing, Oregon, and Texas, are yet unsung. Yet America is a poem in our eyes; its ample geography dazzles the imagination, and it will not wait long for metres.[1]

Emerson but touched on this hope, in a paragraph rarely con-crete amid the abstractions of his "The Poet." Perhaps, he seems to suggest, if the poet abandoned the cosmic search and stayed his reach to what was near at hand he might do better. Emerson had still to wait a decade for the candidate to come forward for that high office. The man, of course, was Walt Whitman.

Walt Whitman had not arrived at his resolve all at once. He knew his own limitations, had dabbled in this and that, had read in no systematic fashion and was without formal education. But he was not to be discouraged, and in this final self-confidence, unwarranted as it might be, he too was American. Emerson, he said, brought him to a boil; and no doubt the Quaker inheritance and the Emer-sonian encouragement to a complete self-trust made his effort possi-ble. The simple, untutored, naive, democratic Walt Whitman would fill the breach and announce the common man and his endless potential in a land of always opening horizons. By the time Walt got around to his first publication under the new resolve, his vision was already becoming blurred by the clouds of a hastening civil war, during which he turned aside to test in fraternal aid on the battlefields his doctrine of the simple, unified man. After the war came the disillusionment, the suspicion that the rectitude of the early republic was being smothered in decay and corruption and the greed of postwar competition. Yet Walt hammered away for the rest of his life to round out his vision, sustained by a certainty that he could not wholly fail.

[1] Emerson, "The Poet," *Works,* II, 40–41.

He had first, however, to frame certain resolutions, in the direction of the selfsame birthright of freedom from the past and its traditions. He must never quote; he must avoid all poetic similes, making reference to actual things only, rivers, persons, real things and not the pictures of things; and especially he must find a language and a rhythm closer to natural speech than any before his time, rhythms that would "break forth loosely as lilacs on a bush." He must draw all from himself, a sample man, without reservations.

Back of these resolves lay certain general ideas, largely to be found in embryo in Emerson's essays but reinforced by a certain personal equipment, one might almost say, a lack of equipment. Above all, he must be unhampered by outside influences not of his own constitution, not of his own country and his countrymen. This he announced, as quoted above, in the opening stanza of his "Song of Myself": to leave all schools and creeds in abeyance, and to allow nature to speak through him, with the original energy and impulse, without hindrance, whatever the hazard. Here we recall not only the Transcendentalist urgings to self-reliance, but also Cooper's ingenuous innocent on the outposts of colonial society, Jefferson's statement that no one had ever determined his opinions for him, Thoreau's fifteen years of struggle to rid himself of an academic rhetoric, Emerson's scholar and his resolve to be free to the point of accepting no hindrance that did not arise out of his own constitution. Whitman shared this longing for a true and native note. He had no wish to lose himself in scholastic debates, old arguments, ancient philosophies—indeed, he had no head for such.

It is useless to seek in Whitman a consistent philosophy. In another land a man of his limitations would never have considered assuming the role of a national voice. Nevertheless, if he were to speak for all men, the humble and the voiceless, he must speak for and from himself, must rely on a dredging of his own being for his materials. The world about him he accepted as he found it, seeing in all a kind of rightness as it was, in a vaguely pantheistic cosmos which included the rightness of common humanity, equal, democratic, fortunate to be in the one human society that held forth a promise to all. Perhaps more determinant in his program than he could know was an extraordinary physical sensitivity to every minutest manifestation of living things, sight and sound, man and nature, and an amazing empathy with all in nature:

> Leaves stiff or drooping in the fields,
> And brown ants in the little wells beneath them,
> And mossy scabs of the worm fence, heap'd stones,
>   elder, mullein and poke-weed.

Above all, Whitman was the champion of people, all the voiceless people in history, those manipulated and led, for the most part, by men who did not believe in men. In "Song of Myself" he proclaims:

> Through me many long dumb voices,
> Voices of interminable generations of prisoners and slaves,
> Voices of the diseas'd and despairing and of thieves and dwarfs,
> . . . Through me forbidden voices.

"Long enough," he announced in *Democratic Vistas*, "have the People been listening to poems in which common humanity, deferential, bends low, humiliated, acknowledging superiors. But America listens to no such poems." [2]

Walt's poems were originally less of the frontier than of the city and country of his own Atlantic coastal area. But as his sense of mission grew, and as he added some travel farther afield, he expanded to the demand for a continental poet. The new poet of America, he wrote in 1856, "spans between them [Atlantic and Pacific] from east to west and reflects what is between them"; and he looked to the newer west to justify him. He sang the song of Pioneers, O Pioneers, taking up the task from the halting, elder races: "Still be ours the diet hard, and the blanket on the ground."

---

[2] Whitman, *Democratic Vistas, Complete Prose Works*, p. 238.

He crossed the continent in imagination in his "Passage to India"; and in long inventories he recorded the endless diversity of American occupations and energies. Always his starting point was the American scene and soil, the American experience.

Much might be written, therefore, of Whitman's use of the native scene and setting. Yet almost all might have remained diffuse and wordy, without a true example of his best powers, had there not occurred in his central period, amid his collecting from first-hand experience the knowledge of men warring and dying on the battle-fields, an opportunity for one magnificent poem such as could never have been written by any other. That poem is "When Lilacs Last in the Dooryard Bloom'd," a major triumph of his method, and a truly native piece.

The rapid rise of the Lincoln legend was surely in part, even aside from his martyrdom, enhanced by the fact that he so thoroughly embodied in his personal history the symbolic native American, product of the New World and its frontiers, the backwoodsman, rail splitter, even onetime Indian fighter, self-taught, risen from poverty and physical labor to the highest position in the land. He had the virtues of Natty Bumppo, Daniel Boone, Thomas Jefferson, and Andrew Jackson; and even if this national portrait was in part the work of political campaign literature, there was enough in the real man to give credence to it.

Lincoln was formed intellectually on Thomas Jefferson. His reading, though limited, had been done intensively and thoughtfully. A practical, independent man, he had, in his own words, to test each new idea by bounding it east, west, north, and south. He was also a brooding, even a melancholy man, uncertain of his ancestry, convinced early that his destiny was a solitary one, acquainted from birth with the forest, prairie, and river solitudes of a new frontier. Whatever his limitations, he was eminently fitted, therefore, to represent the American product; and in time even the Brahmins of New England, Emerson and Lowell, accepted his thoroughly

native quality and recognized in it an achievement of a native sort.
"He was thoroughly American," said Emerson in a memorial
speech in 1865, "had never crossed the sea . . . a quite native,
aboriginal man . . . no aping of foreigners, no frivolous accomplishments, Kentuckian born, working on a farm, a flatboatman . . . a
country lawyer." [3]

There is evidence, internal and otherwise, that Whitman thought
long about his poem, and that the result is a compound of the poet's
love of his native land and of the figure from its inland soil. The
poem might be one upon some nameless, wholly American friend,
for Lincoln himself is not mentioned by name or by title as Presi-
dent, though the national reach of the funeral train would scarcely
be mistaken for any other's passing. But even that train is subdued,
rendered microscopic, as it were, amid the endless lanes and old
woods, the grass and the fields of grain through which it passes. All
of Whitman's symbols are drawn from unspoiled nature and from
the simple people who stand silent and nameless in their grief.
There is no mention of capital city, or of parade, military pomp
and circumstance, titles or ranks, church rituals, or even the familiar
Biblical references to a time of death. Instead, all is steeped in the
scenery of America, "the varied and ample land"; the perfumes of
winds meeting on the far-reaching prairies, or touching the breasts
of rivers "with a wind dapple here and there, with ranging hills";
the humble scenes of workshops and of working men returning to
their homes; the "south and north in the light of the sun, the sun
and stars over all"; and all a part of "the large unconscious scenery
of my land with its lakes and forests." One seems to look down from
some high vantage point upon America, the land, and its grief.

And yet the land is *not* in grief—that is the discovery—but serene
and acceptant as the train passes through it, through the forests and
lanes with the humble violets, through the fields of grain, the or-

[3] Emerson, "Abraham Lincoln," *Works,* XI, 308.

chards in blossom, and the little towns where the people stand with uplifted faces. The poet, seeking to resolve the puzzle, turns to the swamp and the deep forests where the shy thrush sings, and where, in time, he arrives at a praise of death, his own acceptance, even as the humble folk along the way stand silently in their acceptance of the ways of living and dying.

The thrush, the solitary bird of nature's depths, is perhaps less the symbol of the poet than the voice of the land responding to the interpreting poet. Deep into the lonely swamp the poet, too, must go, and alone he must try his song, for it is to be more than an elegy; it is to be a clue to the meaning of death within the pattern of nature. It is also to be the voice of America, the new opportunity, which has produced this native son as if in token of its promise. The poet must seek not only escape from the artificialities of cities and formalities and an assumed grief, but the very meaning of the New World and its renewed knowledge of nature. The purification of his song is a necessity, an imperative if he would envision the full meaning of the man and the hour.

Armed with the vision of his native land and its sweep and grandeur, which he calls the picture to be hung on the memorial walls, the poet listens once more to the song of the solitary thrush, the shy "gray-brown bird,"

> With pure deliberate notes filling the night,
> Loud in the pines and cedars dim.

And in this dim, wholly native setting begins the lyric, "Come lovely and soothing death," capturing at last the reconciliation of man, and land, and nature's serene whole. "Praised be the fathomless universe," for which "the sights of the open landscape and the high-spread sky are fitting." This lyric is followed by the vision of war and its thousands of silent slain, the grief of those who remain, the threnody of the aftermath of war, America, north and south. Yet the deaths of these was "not as was thought," for it is the living who grieve, not the dead. The poem ends as it began, though with vast, new connotations,

> Lilac and star and bird twined with the chant of my soul,
> There in the fragrant pines and the cedars dusk and dim.

Is this poem marred or narrowed by the omission of the traditional trappings of the elegy down through English poetry? On the contrary; it is, as it were, swept clean and clear of conventional clichés by the prairie breezes, the grassy lanes, and the violets in the woods, the song of the solitary thrush. The tribute to the native son from the very center of the new experiment, with all that this must imply for the poet in search of the meaning of his own land, his own confidences, has been but a sprig of lilac, a native, farmyard flower. And for memorial, the vision of farmhouses over the face of a democratic land, and people standing in silent bereavement at the little railway stations—working folk who have dropped their toil to look up, not bowing, at the train as it passes, their grief in their eyes and their silence; the corpses of the many battlefields, men from the commonest homes of the land; and the song of the shyest of native birds, singing apart in the deepest recesses of forest and swamp. As to where it all fits into a formal philosophy, a creed, who cares? It was what Whitman had wanted to say, out of his own belief and urge for the poet of America. At last the new land, its long reaches of nature untamed and of nights and days of solitude, had found a voice. America had its poet.

part 3 VARIATIONS ON A THEME

Until we found out that it was ourselves
We were withholding from our land of living . . .

—Robert Frost, "The Gift Outright"

xi. The Fading Frontier

It was never quite said—that wonder of the New World and the dream of a new kind of man. Perhaps now it never could be said; for even while the New Englanders were making the effort to comprehend and Whitman to give it form and body, the evidence was fading. It might be, as Emerson had said, that Europe stopped at the Appalachians and beyond was America, and hence it behoved the American poet and essayist to consider closely the significance of the new materials at his disposal. Yet the conflict between the states, the older eastern states, was followed by an intense concentration in the north on a new prosperity, and in the south by a brooding upon a lost past, while the west drew off the youthful energies of both in its own kind of exploitation of mineral, cattle, and oil resources. True, the "west" became a boisterous cliché of expansiveness; but where now was the far call of the unexplored horizon, the freedom of the trapper and mountain man, the life among the primitive savages? All was giving way to the vast midwestern American average, the uniformity of little towns that duplicated in ever shabbier form the patterns left behind —that vast average that later writers would castigate for an unbroken dullness, a shallow conformity, a petty materialism, and an almost total absence of esthetic awareness.

"History," said Henry James, writing in 1879 on Hawthorne and the limitations of American material for the novelist, "as yet, has left in the United States but so thin and so impalpable a deposit that we very soon touch the hard substratum of nature; and [he characteristically adds] nature herself, in the Western World, has the peculiarity of seeming rather crude and immature." [1] The newer mood for the next era was here forecast, the mood of disillusionment with the American scene.

Yet the American, for all his cultural limitations, knew with a certainty that he had participated in a historic moment, a folk movement without a parallel in modern times, and that knowledge owed little to books or nature mysticism. The literary awareness of the frontier had been the work of bookish men, not authentic frontiersmen, albeit men of books who had grasped the prevailing mood of their countrymen and attempted to give it a voice. Only Whitman, perhaps, stood with a foot in each camp, the true intermediary, though not strictly representative of either.

The odd thing about these earlier manipulators of the frontier symbol and metaphor was that most of them were neither frontiersmen trying to give voice to their knowledge nor travellers reporting on their observations, but booklovers and library writers attempting to evaluate and assimilate a national experience which they saw correctly enough as something new in history, something available to the creators of a native literature. Europeans and descendants of Europeans, aware of their past, since their formal education was almost wholly within that inheritance, they felt compelled nevertheless to examine their New World inheritance as well and to assert their discovery that men could live without the hallowed traditions. This the frontier symbolized. But while they groped for the new

---

[1] Henry James, *Hawthorne*, p. 12.

materials and their significance, the frontier was going, becoming secondhand, and would finally be reduced to a form of lip service ensconced in familiar phrases like "the pioneer virtues," "the American way," or "new frontiers." After its official demise in 1890 the frontier survived only in scattered pockets, or, like the bison, moved northward to Alaska or Canada. The "new frontiers" of a recent presidential message sounded thinly in the urban air.

For the frontiersman and the western inheritor of his setting, the frontier was neither theory nor abstraction; it was experience, it was memory, in the muscles, the knowledge of the walker afoot, the food eaten, the habits enforced, and the thinking apart, the pride and the confidence won of hard testings such as could never let the knower rest content within the conventional categories. It was, also, a white man's knowledge, as Cooper had said, for it took almost nothing from Indian myth and legend beyond a few place names and a kind of respect for Indian skills in nature and Indian stoicism in the face of pain.

The proof that the frontier was no form of initiation rites or pseudo myth (those lures for amateur scholarship without experience on the land) is that it bred no ritual, no creed, no organized society or club. All that would come, as is the way with romanticism, after the reality had faded. In this absence of definition it shared with, perhaps even encouraged, the transcendentalist freedom even from one another. "I charge you," says Whitman, "to leave all free as I have left all free." The initiation of the frontier was but the sharing of the perils of the unknown and the pull of the open spaces where a man was to be tested as individual man. It was simplicity itself, like the fraternity of those who knew the trenches of World War I, whose members needed no mumbo jumbo or secret grip but only experiences shared. The common knowledge in both cases was masculine, physical, immediate, a mostly wordless knowledge, spoken of sparingly—the boaster talked others out of confidence in him— and it was not contingent on what the literary men might say.

All this the literary fraternity groped for in that remote Jacksonian era. But all this was long ago; and even as they wrestled with the implications of the open society of the frontier, it was slipping farther away and the skeptic breath of civilization was following hard after. Nevertheless, the European who asserted that America was nothing but factory, smokestack, railroads, and material greed was wrong. The memory was there, both of frontier and of independency, even in those who had not known it literally. The old hunter, leaning on his gun, the pioneer facing the setting sun across the still unplowed grasslands, would have wondered at this Old World misunderstanding, even while he might have sensed an ominous note of prophecy for the future. Deep down the American knew he had touched something real, something close to the human story itself on this planet, forgotten though it might be elsewhere. "The wilderness is near, as well as dear, to every man," said Thoreau; and he dismissed even the ancient heroes, the sacred names, as "now only the subtilest imaginable essences, which would not stain a morning sky." [2] Such it was to feel the freshness of the American experience, the renewal of the youth of the race; and its connotations were a compound of the original drive to found Utopias and Edens in an unspoiled setting, and the equally radical discovery of the emancipation of the average individual.

It would appear unnecessary to belabor this actuality of the American experience. Yet one runs across sentences like the following, here from the Spiller-Thorpe *Literary History of the United States:* "Thus," say the writers of the particular chapter, "by grace of Jean Jacques Rousseau, our poets and novelists came to see the West as a strange but beautiful land of vast spaces where a man could live freely." [3] We must protest; this is a kind of academic jargon born of a passion for "tracing influences." Plainly, neither the spaces

[2] Thoreau, *A Week, Writings,* I, 223.
[3] R. E. Spiller, W. Thorpe, *et al.* (eds.), *Literary History of the United States,* II, 777.

nor the frontiersman's response to them existed by the grace of any scrivener, much less a European one, and surely not by that of Rousseau, scarcely known west of Philadelphia. No, the original knowledge was born of the solitary foot-before-foot striding toward the unknown, and from the mouths of a few whose slow trudging advance found expression, to be caught up later in the imagination of poets and novelists eager to explore a native theme. It would be far truer to say that Rousseau and Chateaubriand found their themes by the grace of the discovery of America and its thunderous echo on the shores of the Old World: and where not in America, Rousseau discovered his idyllic settings in Locke and Wolff and Lucretius and the Mediterranean past.

Today the old themes of nature as inspiration and the virtues of solitude become an anachronism. We observe in our setting less evidence of man exulting in his natural rights than of man in "the lonely crowd," the organization man and his pitiable subservience, the crack in the picture window, and the passing of individuality in a general conformity, threatening to congeal into a narrow provincialism in the face of the new. Ours is an urban society, and the old theme shrinks to a monotony of "westerns"; or it hides within a synthetic tourism, a chamber of commerce ballyhoo about old-timers, the annual replicas of frontier bars and ladies of easy virtue and the quick draw. But let us not be contemptuous of our moment of seeing nature plain and clear.

How have the old themes fared in a twentieth-century setting? Are they doomed to fade in a shallow melodrama of screen and television? What substitutes, if any, have been proposed for a lost innocence? Do we find in our major twentieth-century writers any echoes of this native past?

On the literary level a goodly number of writers have, indeed, endeavored to recapture that past in realistic terms, to scrutinize the legend, the sentiment, and the melodrama of heroism and violence. One thinks of such serious works as Rölvaag's *Giants in the Earth*

or Marie Sandoz' *Old Jules,* in which the Old World comers make
their adjustments, or of Richter's *The Sea of Grass,* Guthrie's *The
Way West,* or the work of Frank Dobie, in which the past is reconstructed with fidelity to its being. This is the way it was, they
try to tell us, with an urgency that admits how much it meant to the
past, how much it still means to a few, how regretful they are because of its passing. Yet these books resemble historical documenta-
tion more than great fiction; and the likelihood is that the newer
generation will lose the touch, failing to distinguish the genuine
from the make-believe.

A little story by John Steinbeck perhaps best suggests the combination of simplicity and the sense of past worth that rarely found
voice in literature. In his "Leader of the People," [4] an old man, a
bore to his children, finds in his small grandson a willing listener, at
least long enough for the old man to unburden his memories of the
past and his pride in a personal participation. He had, literally, led
a party across the western plains and mountains. This had been his
great moment, for it was "a job for men." Had he led a war mission
so great a distance, the reader might observe, his name would be
in history; but since it was a conquest of space, of land, of half a
continent, and a responsibility for common folk seeking a home,
a leadership against attack, thirst, and starvation, he was forgotten.
But it was not Indians or adventure that stirred the old man. "It was
westering . . . it was movement and westering." And that movement
dignified an otherwise commonplace man by the very fact of re-
sponsible participation in it. Here was a modest, yet wholly warranted claim of a simple man to his place in history. He offered no
melodrama of desperado or killer, no boast, but simply a right to
recognition, a man of humble but respectable antecedents who had
conducted himself honorably and with credit in a position of leadership. This the old man could feel with conviction, even though

[4] John Steinbeck, "The Leader of the People," *The Long Valley.*

he bored others because he lacked the dishonesty to embellish his
tale or the discipline to give it adequate expression, and because
he lacked now a place in society. All he possessed was the actuality
of knowledge, at first hand, truthfulness to incident, achievement
which dignified him to himself.

Others have attempted to capture the reality in prose and poem.
Struthers Burt, whose western retreat in the Teton country of
Wyoming entered into a novel (*The Delectable Mountains*) and a
book in the river series (*Powder River*), tried to capture the essence
of the region—"a dreaming, disdainful country . . . as if it looked
across the present, not noticing it, to a future as lonely as its past." [5]
In these long vistas Burt perceived the same remoteness from man's
self-concern that Melville discovered in his ocean voyages; though
Burt adds the more modern note of man's impermanence.

Thomas Hornsby Ferril, third-generation Coloradoan and Denver
poet, complained some twenty years ago in a *Saturday Review* article
that western writing was forever being "devitalized by a low-grade
mysticism dictated by landscape." [6] Too much western writing, he
said, proceeds on the assumption that there is something mystical
about the magnitude of western mountains and valleys which demands that the writer create superhuman males to match the landscape. The fact is, he asserted, and rightly, that good poetry is made
out of concrete experience, not of loose ecstasy, and that in good
literature it is man, not scenery, that is central. For this reason, said
Ferril, many bare recordings of early travellers contain in their
sparse prose more poetry than is found in western verse.

Ferril's own method of escaping the pitfalls is to view these uplifted ranges through the lenses of geological realities, seeing them
not as timeless and supernatural, but as subject, like all things, to
change, growth, decay. Thus man's mind acts to subdue scenery to

[5] Struthers Burt, *The Delectable Mountains*, p. 155.
[6] Thomas Hornsby Ferril, "Writing in the Rockies," *The Rocky Mountain Reader*,
ed. Ray B. West, pp. 395–403.

his own insights; and by the power of imagination he binds past, present, and future, and blends the works of man into the large rhythms of the landscape.

Nature, that is, is the all-absorbing reality, the persistent theme, not as enemy or outsider but as the natural home of man, as it is of animal and machine. Thus, writing a poem on the remnants of old Fort Laramie on the Platte, he remarks, "Fort Laramie is nature now"; and of those buried there: "Any man is natural/ as a prairie dog . . ./ Or a wind that blows a mountain down." This last phrase is not mere extravagance, for any western geologist will show you hollows where once stood hills and mountains reduced by the elements amid the more resistant deposits. Again, observing the delphinium that pushes up through a rotting plank floor in an abandoned cabin, he writes:

> This is Wyoming walking in,
> I said, through an open door. . . .
> And the roof is a thing the sun shines through
> To make Wyoming flowers blue.[7]

Or, viewing an abandoned Model-T Ford on the Cheyenne plains as but an artifact, like one of Thoreau's Indian arrowheads, he sees it as the starting point for a new legend of a past that once was:

> The dry wind out of Wyoming might have whispered:
> "Today is going to be long long ago." [8]

Thus Wyoming and Colorado, their names but political labels, take on the patina of time and a poetic coloring. To their own inhabitants, these states commonly arouse connotative images of far, high plains or austere, distant ranges unlikely ever to be touched by human spoilation. The reader of Ferril, however, learns to see them

---

[7] Thomas Hornsby Ferril, *New and Selected Poems*, p. 93.
[8] *Ibid.*, p. 162.

as "the solvent mountains going home to the oceans"; [9] and by means of this geologic perspective, man becomes one with the silent dignity of nature that surrounds him, without the necessity of self-inflation, chauvinism, or melodrama. Ferril, indeed, has done something to put the great west once more into a truer perspective, and man within his landscape.

Walter Van Tilburg Clark, confronted similarly with the problem of the western setting, also rejects the conventional sentimentalities, even while motivated by a strong and personal sense of his native land. His argument is that the true antagonist in this setting is not another man with shooting irons but the setting itself, either as a background which permits the reduction of human conflicts to the sharp, the concrete, and individual clash, as in *The Oxbow Incident,* where individual character stands out starkly, unable to find shelter in a mass anonymity; or as the dominant, ever present fact, itself a character in the conflict, as in the more mystical *The Track of the Cat.* In this latter work, Clark risked the overt symbolism of the mountain cat as a representation of something which man, for all his resoluteness, can never subdue—the impersonal scheme of nature, perhaps. He imparted a very real sense of terror before the elemental, as the single man is pitted against wilderness, winter snows, and the beast. Yet his novel was not so simply man against nature as this brief comment would imply, for the man is motivated also by the notion of what it is to be man, to assert his essence as man even as the cat asserts its way of life. The man has come to this confrontation in part as a consequence of his solitude in the natural setting.

Certain twentieth-century critics, mainly eastern, however, have not been moved by this western note. Edmund Wilson, for example, writing in the *New Yorker* for May 20, 1945, complained that Clark, Steinbeck, Saroyan are "too easy going and good natured . . . always dissolving into an even sunshine, always circumventing by ample

[9] *Ibid.,* p. 7.

detours what one expects to be sharp or direct." [10] It is difficult, it
appears, to treat of deserts and mountains in western terms, the instinctive response of the westerner to his setting, without arousing
eastern suspicions. The conflicts of an urban society must be socially
determined, corporation-conditioned, sex-involved, tense, and localized. Can the west have a literature of its own, great and impressive?

[10] It is only fair to add that Mr. Wilson urges the west to produce "a literature of
its own appropriate to its temper and climate, and almost as independent of New
England and New York and the South as it is of current fashions in Europe."

xii. Not from Landscape, Not from Flight[1]

THE QUERY might be framed somewhat as follows: why has not the west produced its national classic, its great American novel, its master in the field of fiction? Why, alone of American regions, has this one, so vast in size, so unique in character, lagged both in the amount and the quality of its fictional output?

To reply with a just impartiality calls for a deliberative judgment and tact. The implications that underlie such a query, the unexamined assumptions that lie behind it, should not perturb us. Eastern critics, like their European counterparts, have been known to mistake their own habits for universals. The great west is what the Atlantic coast once was to Europe, a new region from which it is assumed that only novelty and not power is to be expected. What, indeed, is a classic? And how surely were those now accepted as such recognized as classics in their own day?

Nevertheless, we may as well reply bluntly at the outset that from

[1] This chapter, with some revisions, is reprinted from the Union College *Symposium*, I (Spring, 1962), 15–19.

our present vantage point there appear to be no modest Melvilles, no sensitive Jamesians or brooding Faulkners hiding in the mountain canyons or patiently waiting their day of discovery in the mining camps and oil fields. That there are western writers deserving of recognition we might willingly maintain; and it is hoped that no injustice is done them if for the purposes of this chapter they are passed over in silence in a consideration of what their problems may be.

It would be too easy, at this point, to paraphrase Jefferson's plea for patience; [2] for though the west has existed in a communal sense a briefer time than had Jefferson's Virginia in 1784 (Indians were staging sporadic rallies even so late as seventy and eighty years ago), time moves more swiftly now, and the excuse would not convince. It would be too facile, and hackneyed besides, to point to the not-distant labors of settlement, the sparseness of population, the marginal nature of much of the land and climate, semiarid and high, and never likely to see a concentrated population aside from a few favored centers. Half the continental United States lies west of Omaha; nevertheless, aside from the Pacific coastal areas and a few intermediate exceptions, it is the national region most likely to remain thinly populated. The central industries may long remain mining, cattle raising, prospecting for oil and new minerals, and catering to the tourist trade. Nor is this west a single, homogeneous region. The states known as the southwest, bordering on Mexico and sharing a Spanish-Mexican culture, embrace a region twice the size of France. Six or seven further states encompass the Rocky Mountain heights from Mexico to the majestic Canadian Rockies; and even the western parts of the trans-Mississippi plains states often look westward in their psychology and share more than a little with the central Canadian provinces. There is also the great northwest, and, of course, always California, embracing Hollywood and Las Vegas, Nevada.

---

[2] As quoted in Chapter V.

But we are discussing literature; and literature on the grand scale has always been preceded by ground-level labors and the economics of some established leisure, as well as some cultural stability against which the writer can rebel. Sophistication demands that some audience be relatively prosperous, even if the author dwell in marginal anxiety. Even on the Atlantic coast, where settlement began with migrating Englishmen already in the age of Shakespeare, there was little literature to command respect until merchants, country gentlemen, lawyers, and schools achieved something like security.

Apologies, however plausible, end by being evasive. Great literature, after all, is where you find it, and emerges not from landscape, not from geographical contours, but from the minds and emotions of a few gifted men and women. It is not to be summoned by group resolutions or by chamber of commerce appeals. Nor is the truly classic in literature ever solely regional in significance. Not the accidents of environment alone but human dilemmas appropriate to their given settings determine the depth of a literature. Who, then, is to determine where the concept "regional" ends and the individual contribution begins? And what does the interpreter interpret? Not scenery, not landscape for their own sakes; for these, however intrusive, however awesome, are but the setting for the human beings involved in human problems. These problems are set in part by their own society, in part by their own personal rejection of that society and its total finality for their lives.

Consider for a moment, by way of example, the literature of the classic day of Russia, a land of great steppes and lonely wastes. That literature came from a small segment of Russian society, an intelligentsia bred, at least superficially, on the literature of Western Europe. It was the work of writers passionate in protest, violent, highly verbal within a rigid social scheme, the violence of rebellious wills gesturing against a formal repression. The impossibility of reconciliation between extremes imparted to that literature of a brief period an intensity of feeling that moves us still, across all the differences of social milieu and language. Landscape entered, if at all, only incidentally. Our American west could never duplicate such a literature, for the autocratic society of the tsars is unknown to us.

We approach, it may be, the crux of the matter. Western appeals to scenery or to the synthetic circuses of frontier days are largely irrelevant and need not detain us longer. The fact is that the over-simplifications of frontier saloons, ladies of easy virtue, and cowtown clashes were long ago exhausted as themes. Action in them is too swift, too impulsive and adolescent in origin to be subject to mature treatment; and the consequences, essentially shallow, are too easily tossed over the shoulder as the hero evades them by riding off to new adventures. A sentimental nostalgia for this elemental past is of little use to those seeking esthetic maturity. The argument of Hamlin Garland, for example, that the prairies encouraged broad concepts and the winds of the west gave power and penetration, and the forests added breadth of intellect, must be assigned to a lingering and already dated romanticism.

Other regions of America, in their own time, have flowered into bursts of literary vitality, but not on these immature terms. New England first rode the crest in a re-examination of its own past and an awareness of a new day on the horizon. The south felt the impact of a romantic era, and later a revival in a protest against the loss of old values. And how recently the middle west arose to challenge the whole country: *Poetry, A Magazine of Verse,* Edgar Lee Masters, Sherwood Anderson, Sinclair Lewis, Sandburg, Hemingway, and a host of lesser names, as there must always be if creative energies are to flourish. Where is that middle region today? Almost voiceless, it would seem, replacing H. L. Mencken's South as the Sahara of the Bozarts, and voiceless for a similar reason, an unwillingness to question a static present. The protests of these writers are dated now; but there had to be the revolt against the long aridity and the pitiful sameness of the little Winesburgs and Zeniths of the turn of the century. Perhaps one day the far west will flex its literary muscles in the national arena, though there arise the moans of the offended legend of the eternal frontier.

Let us imagine, then, some novel laid in Denver or Seattle, two expanding regional centers. At once it will be perceived either that the central conflict and style will differ little from those of a novel laid in New York or Chicago, or that the people of the western city will be found to act by some code or custom that departs in some observable way from those of the eastern habit. If the latter, we must ask what is that code, that manner, and is it western, and does that fact in any degree determine the quality and the pattern of the conflict within the novel? If we find no crucial differences, then the American novel may as well come from one city as another. And, indeed, in our monolithic society, especially insofar as it is urban, differences do tend to become pallid or minor. Nevertheless, let us take a second look at the western setting.

The first obvious remark will be that the west has long been, especially for eastern writers, a kind of fictional escape-land—flight, that is, from urban tensions, from the dilemmas of a more sophisticated milieu, or from oppressive family ties and competitive businesses without creative stimulus. If the figure of an Atlantic coast novel touches the west, it is usually to treat it as a vacation land, a refuge, a means of easier divorce, a temporary passing-through in the interim of personal conflicts, themselves localized in the east, even in Europe. Thus the west lingers as a setting for the renewal of the human spirit for the crisis back home, or the recovery of the creative urge. One has but to think of Owen Wister, eastern born, or of Willa Cather's *The Song of the Lark* or *The Professor's House*, in each of which the central character turns to the mountain region for renewal. As far back as Bret Harte's imported sentimentality, through Willa Cather or Struthers Burt's *The Delectable Mountains*, to Steinbeck's guileless *paisanos* and Saroyan's happy innocents, the western setting has been utilized as the symbol of freedom from conventional restraints, a happy irresponsibility, or, in its more austere solitudes, as surcease from anxiety, a stretching of the muscles, and a renewal of the will to live. This is humanly fine. But as such it is not enough for a great regional literature. It too nearly parallels the romantic age of nature worship, or the American tourist's delight in the baroque monuments of Europe at the price of a total ignorance of their cost in European history and politics. If the west were to be limited to this contribution alone, however pleasant in its way, we might well despair of a literature of power from its inhabitants.

We recall Edmund Wilson's complaint that western authors tend to minimize human tensions, to smooth out conflicts and evade issues, to permit of too cheerful solutions, and so to end in second-rate novels. Literary greatness, it is true, does seem to gravitate toward the soberer hues and tragedy does rate above melodrama and romance; Hawthorne and Melville may well outlast the milder transcendentalism of their era. We cannot wholly dismiss Edmund Wilson's comment, or attribute it solely to a twentieth-century pre-dilection for anxiety, neurosis, and the self-pity of the hollow men.

Let us suggest that a certain kind of primitivism does linger in the American west; not, to be sure, the self-conscious primitivism of modern art, but a genuine, lingering romanticism, touched with nostalgia for something lost, plus the happy indifference of the out-door man to self-criticism and self-doubt. For the older west, though traditionally associated with physical trial, endurance and hardship, and a kind of toughness, did at the same time encourage a youthful-ness of spirit. The west has been, or has been assumed to be, some-what easier on men and women if we refer only to the kind of nervous tensions, pressures, breadlines, economic blind alleys, and social rejections that prevail in much modern urban living. Salinger's *Catcher in the Rye,* for instance, is wholly urban and would be unimaginable from the states of Idaho or Wyoming, as would, let us say, Ralph Ellison's [The] *Invisible Man.* The west, historically, has always implied the chance to move on, to refuse the final despair of economic or social defeat, the ultimate in the competitive stresses of great industrial and financial centers. This is not to say that exploitation of human resources has not too often accompanied the story of the western rise. It has, indeed; even so, the nomadic impulse and remedy is strong. Nor has the westerner felt the same burden of old families and the introverted resentments of offspring. The westerner's role, slipping into the past though that role may now be, has been traditionally that of a denial of the weight and burden of older societies.

The self-pitying outcries that stain the pages of a metropolitan fiction, or the brooding regional guilt and defeat that hang over southern literature, seem foreign to the western setting. "What is all the talk about? Why don't they do something about it?" the western college student will sometimes ask his instructor, impatient with the too-verbal, too-ego-centered, too-assertive-because-insecure product of the pavements of the east. To reply that the western youth might disintegrate even more rapidly in that environment is beside the point and is not necessarily proved, judging by the amazing proportion of successful Americans whose roots are in the midwestern and western soil. The point is simply that the westerner, in his own environment, is less likely to know the same stresses, and so tends to react somewhat less tensely. The western youth, putting his pen to paper, will often seem less articulate, less literate, that is, less sophisticatedly verbal, than his eastern counterpart; he is also more likely to come up with sentimentality of place, the clichés of the frontier past, or the violence of melodrama instead of an exploration of the more tortuous mazes of neurosis, that is, with action over reflection—which is to say, with the surface of literature.

The west, it becomes clear, is not the most natural setting for the classical novel of manners. The west, like America itself, was built on escape—escape from Europe originally, from restrictive institutions and patterns, from the hard lot of serfdom and peasantry, from despair within and depression without. All the genealogical research in America but reinforces the fact that our origins were uniformly humble and that the first comers imported less the habits of authority than the resentments of the underprivileged. The prevailing pattern was dissent, not conformity. The satisfactions sought were far less cultural than economic, less the disciplines of great art and literature than the hope of a home free from interference. The very clichés of European condescension toward American origins substantiate not only the fact but the American suspicion that average man in Europe must have been more cheaply regarded, and that the New World must have appealed to him as a chance to recover or prove an individual manhood and worth.

The question, then, as has been said above, has always been: can great art emerge from humble folk as they prosper, can it emerge from individualism, dissent, flight from tradition? Whitman, as we know, asserted that it could and must. It takes not much insight, however, to see that individualism without talent is not enough, that freedom without the creative urge will remain unproductive. There must always be the renewed grappling with the basic human dilemmas, those which are forever inescapable and from which the traditions themselves originally took their rise. If the west has in some degree evaded these, or cast them in immature terms, its literature will remain incomplete.

It falls to the lot of all human beings to encounter the frictions of living with one another; to know those subtle gradations among people which make for upper and lower and in-between; to feel the irritants of social inequality, the unrelenting offishness of the secure who wish to remain secure and of the "superior" who would prove their superiority by the trivia of a social "know-how"; and to experience, in consequence of such exacerbations, the small angers of the excluded and the rejected, the rationalizations by which they must combat the evidence that they do not "belong." In old societies these levels are relatively fixed and strong to survive even revolutions. The emphasis in such societies must be historically on the resignation of the mass of people, the reiterated lesson of "proper stations." These assumptions the American has never accepted, even from the start, simply because he did not have to. Hence his conclusion that they were imposed, not natural to mankind. The note of the American, especially as he turned westward, has been indifference to status symbols, and the preferred gospel of the innate, at least the potential, equality of all, the quick rise of peasant and immigrant to property holder, and his rapid entry into the ranks of professional people and office status. The word "peasant," indeed, has never found a place in the American vocabulary.

It was these same veiled subtleties in older societies, so pervasive, so difficult, even esoteric, for the uninitiated, that attracted Henry James to his art and made it appear that he had all but renounced the vulgarities of his native land. Yet James, though his countrymen did not always suspect it, and though it may seem remote from the present discussion, remained American still.

In an earlier novel, *The American,* James presents the conflict in plain, if not even simplified, terms. His American, Christopher (discoverer) Newman (new man from the New World), a man of no particular background yet possessing the freedom of wealth, quite confident of his own resources, at heart an honorable man, pits his will against that of a titled French family. His hope is to carry off to America the daughter, Claire de Cintré (a name not so immediately translatable but, shall we say, a kind of illumination—*claire*—in an arched niche or window—*cintré*—whether of castle or dungeon or both). Her environment is that of a tight, secretive, formalized past, firmly united against the wilful outsider. In the end, partly by this impenetrable unity, partly by his own refusal to take a dishonorable advantage of his knowledge of a family secret, Newman is defeated. But is he, really? The answer must depend on the reader's predilections. Surely, however, the French family of this novel cannot, in any naive sense, be considered a happy one; and, indeed, the American's efforts are partly in the nature of a rescue.

Nor can Claire's withdrawal from all to a convent be equated with the customary American understanding of happiness on the secular level. She has been defeated, whether by her own family or by her own choice of submission to the family's will. The American, in western terms, is still the fortunate one, the one who has escaped the niche in the wall to return to the world of new opportunities, unencumbered by the finespun, introverted distinctions of an entrapped society. Is it fanciful to see James at this stage of his career (and even long later, if you wish, in perhaps his finest novel, *The Ambassadors*) as not wholly committed, after all, to the superiority of old Europe?

Nor are these paragraphs a digression from our main theme if we see how James, and even more markedly a more centrally inspired American writer—say Twain or Hemingway—can refuse, in his greater freedom, to be drawn into the subtleties, the tight social codes, which are not his, and how this refusal makes impossible for the western American writer the true novel of manners, not only of a Jane Austen but even of a Henry James or an Edith Wharton. One has only to read the opening pages of Miss Wharton's *Age of Innocence* to see what could scarcely be done, even yet, by a western writer. Kathleen Norris' *Certain People of Importance,* laid in San Francisco, or Stephen Crane's "The Bride That Came to Yellow Sky," for all its now dated humor, would illustrate a counterpart attempt in the west.

Here is the problem, then: if you take your stand on this none-of-your-finespun-distinctions, your drawing-room-subtleties, your manufactured conflicts, you will be thrown back upon the simplicities of a more primitive code of manners, the violence of physical clashes, of man and muscle, of man against man or man against nature, without the benefits of status and rank and the niceties of a more complicated society. Gain or loss for the free individual, literature will be at any rate the loser in subtlety of plot or refinement of issues in conflict. Polish and subtlety of nuance will yield to speed and action, impulsiveness will replace deliberation, vocabulary will be more direct, more blunt, less discriminating, more responsive to the immediate impulse, more wilful, less introverted. One cannot have it both ways at once. A new arbiter arises, and this one is armed neither with the lorgnette nor the monocled stare at the vulgarities of the new man. It is, instead, one that insists on directness of experience over cumulative tradition. It will, it also happens, be more in tune with a world of prolonged Cold War and the horrors of a too recent memory, a world in which elemental urges push us all to an impatience with the artificialities of a Victorian past. For the conflicts of the novel must always reflect the pressures of the age.

Henry Seidel Canby once wrote a book entitled *Turn West, Turn East,* in which he put Mark Twain against Henry James as best illustrative of the two pulls in American intellectual history, eastward toward Europe, westward toward the rawer frontier. The American way of life, he argued, is a compound of "European culture surprisingly altered by a turn to the West," in consequence of which Americans have either "made themselves new men and women by Western experience," or have tried to become "more civilized by going back for nourishment to the sources of our culture." Nevertheless, in the end, he found certain traits uniting these two figures. Both, he said, "will live in literature by best describing what each called American innocence." [3] Indeed, he found that the two men shared a common code, a moral code of hatred of treachery and preference for integrity, loyalty, intellectual courage, the inclination to grant strangers the qualities they admired in their own countrymen, and the shock at innocence betrayed. If these are the virtues of the older America, they are the product of the more open if more crude society, the more generous if less cultivated environment.

What then is the western writer to aim at? Shall he seek to ape

[3] H. S. Canby, *Turn West, Turn East,* p. xi.

the successes of the past, the more saleable fictional output of the present? He might, it is possible, find a kind of theme by putting the typical westerner against an urban milieu. So far this has been attempted in terms of comedy, even slapstick comedy; it probably offers but a limited field anyway, even though it is what James did with his fellow countrymen and countrywomen and Europe. The fact is, however, that if the western writer wishes to remain true to his own knowledge, his own material, and to retain his personal integrity within his own experience, he may have to accept the likelihood that his characters do not react in every detail in the terms expected by the eastern critic. At the same time, he will have to fight the stereotype of which he is partially the victim, a stereotype created as much by outsiders as by his own area. The old overworked formula demands that western literature connote action and physical conflict, that the characters be laconic, nonverbal, given less to introspection than to sitting on their heels in long silences, though permitted now and then a bit of folk wisdom, perhaps in dialect, or even allowed on occasion to be a bunkhouse reader of Carlyle's *Sartor Resartus* or of Shakespeare and to speak thereafter in a combination of bombast and irony. Such a stereotype imposes on the western book the requirement that a more penetrating character be an imported one from the east.

In the face of such demands the western writer is damned if he does and damned if he doesn't. If he conforms to the stereotype, he is second-rate; if he attempts to pattern himself after some mode more highly touted in the literary centers, he is imitative and second-rate. Yet the day rapidly approaches, if it is not already at hand, when the western writer can emerge from anywhere, equipped with his or her unique way of seeing life, and make the next contribution.

The answer would seem to lie in some conscious declaration of independence from both forces, western stereotype or eastern model, and at the same time, in a recognition that declarations of independence are of small consequence unless followed by the unique next contribution. The western writer will have to examine his own resources, develop his own audience, ponder his own themes, establish his own criteria, be his own interpreter of his own integrity; and beyond all, he will have to have something to say. This is no new prescription. It is, in fact, a kind of rule for all major art striving for birth; and if it paraphrases in some degree Emerson's *American Scholar,* this is but an inevitable repetition, the necessary assertion of new talent, intellect, artistic judgment, insights into human motivations.

What the western writer, then, will need to do is to take himself and his environment with a new seriousness, to examine afresh for weakness or for strength the pattern by which he and his fellow westerners appear to live, and to posit what that code might mean in any extended version over a larger segment of humanity. It is not so much a defense of his own inheritance that he needs as what other major writers have possessed, an enlarged awareness of both what is his own and what is not his own. He must gain perspective on his own region by a wider knowledge and a wider reading than his own locale will provide him. It is worth noting that regional writing with depth has often proceeded from a writer in exile or in a position to view his own from outside. Again, the western writer, admitting the possible handicap of a locale, must sharpen his awareness of the resources of the English language. The inevitable monotony of shock words oft repeated will not suffice to convey a mature protest or a mature portrait of society. And no writer, in the long run, can escape the measuring rod of his command of his own language. Language, too, he must treat with respect.

Every writer, in the words of Joseph Conrad, longs *to make you see.* But see what? And how make you see? These are things the western writer must, in his turn, wrestle with. The point here is that if our western writer begins with provincial boasting or a belligerent localism, his case as artist is lost before he starts. No art comes from a narrow denial of a variant world. The western writer, that is, will study his own inheritance, without timidity before local opinion, and without too much concern about a critical clique on an eastern seaboard. A certain aloofness from either will do him no harm; for all artists live in part on the sufferance of the majority of people, whose attitudes range from mild curiosity, even interest, to open hostility. And if he wants to make you see how life in the west may take its peculiar form, he may well conclude that the motives that prevail for his characters need not parallel those of the asphalt jungles of the great cities, though they may well exhibit human frailty in their own form.

The west, our writer may conclude, has still a substratum of native philosophy, however simplistic. The healing that the great spaces have traditionally supplied, it may appear, is neither that of the psychoanalyst's couch nor of a retreat into a conventional religion; for in that impersonal solitude still possible in the great west—that emptiness where, in the words of J. B. Priestley's *Midnight on the Desert,* "man has not yet been acknowledged," where all is "geology by day and astronomy by night"—the small shrieks of the ego may come to seem trivial, not from the pouting refusal of the beatniks to play the human game, nor yet from the "absurd" of the existentialist *néant,* but from the simple immaturity of playing the part of a childish hurt in the face of nature's calm and indifferent silence. As it does to the infant left alone to cry in the night, there may come to the would-be writer the moment of recognition that wails yield no very solid result and end by being futile; and a step is taken toward a kind of maturity that may, though not wholly articulate, be the equal of the sophistication of literary cocktail parties and literary fads.

Finally, what can be done about this western optimism, this disgraceful cheerfulness and acceptance of the lesser intensity? Wait, one would suppose, for the scar tissue to accumulate. Wait for the deeper tragedies to sear, and the more sensitive crop of writers to arise to evaluate them. When the west catches on to its own loss of youth and the second thoughts of maturity will no longer be denied, we may see the greater western novel. The growing pessimism of Mark Twain's later years is well known and has been the subject of speculation. One source may well have been in his awareness of the passing of the frontier day, the fading of that paradise of escape from social responsibility and convention. Twain delighted in shocking the conventional and the narrowly pious; yet that impulse may have been but the obverse of the shield of inner rebellion against conformity, the frontiersman's impatience with small restraints. With his intelligence, Twain knew that he could never recapture the abandon of Huck Finn, the glorious days of the river pilot, the free frontiers of Nevada and California. He suffered from that knowledge and transferred that malcontent to his doubts about the whole American scene. He hated the deeper suspicion that America, too, must abandon its youth, its unreflective confidence in the national theme of hope, self-reliance, and self-direction on all levels. The United States, he speculated after his circumnavigation of the globe, must someday come to the sorrow and bitterness of Europe, and Europe to the horrors of Asia. Who has yet proved him wrong? The fear behind flight is always the fear of recapture.

Tragedy enough, then, let us say, when the world at large loses the American dream of open opportunity for all men; conflict enough and pain enough, misgivings enough, antagonists enough within and without, when and if the freer American becomes a memory merely, a fading Golden Day taking its turn in the legendary past, when or if its symbolic role as champion of the underprivileged, the asserter of individual worth and dignity, should no longer be viable. It has been argued that democracy was born with the frontier and will pass with it. So it may be if its meaning cannot be transmuted into other terms more pertinent to our own day. And if the west does not defend this heritage, who will?

The shallow west of melodrama and gunplay would be no great loss. The failure to assert before the glass runs out the essential worth of a man, quite apart from institutional or bureaucratic approvals,

might be the last and greatest of tragedies, closing a drama begun
long ago on the shores of the Mediterranean. The western novelist
who could give form and power to such a theme would not be aping
others or bowing merely to the giants of the past. Nor would his
regionalism be local. He might be the voice of half of mankind,
threatened by the grim promises the morrow may hold. His would
be the eternal provincialism of any man, the simple human entity,
speaking out against the eternal injustice of those who forever plot
against their fellows.

To be great literature, his would have to be human literature; and
to be human, it would have to possess the provincialism and the
lack of provincialism of the human story itself.

xiii. A Veneer of Naturalism

IN THE LAST DECADES of the nineteenth
century that flexible word *nature* underwent a new shift. No longer was it
the Puritan term of reproach to the creature man nor the brooding
companion of his deeper thoughts, but now an -ism, a doctrine of a
mechanistic universe in which men are the pawns of impersonal
forces against which they have small or no control. Such a movement could not take place without opposition, to be sure; yet its
touch is upon most subsequent American literature, for its effect
was to bring into high relief the essential romanticism of the older
strains.

Actually, the term *naturalism* has definite limitations as a critical
classification for American writers, for few of them can be brought
to fit neatly into its more rigorous implications; nor is any American
writer so tagged wholly devoid of nonnaturalistic elements. The old
American optimism dies hard, and naturalism could never wholly
tempt the popular taste. For one thing, its doctrine not only affronted
a native optimism, but religion stood opposed to its wholly mechanistic determinism. Man must feel himself to be a participant in all
that concerns him; and soon naturalism in America took on over-

tones of social protest or an urgency to do something against social injustices. If a theory of personal determinism found society one of the forces at work, then let society be reformed for man's improvement. This was not a consistent reply, but neither was a Puritan determinism consistent with man's responsibility.

In the meantime, secondary figures, local-color novelists, nature lovers, and aspiring rhymsters kept alive the more familiar note. In poetry the old vagueness and uplift in the presence of nature sank to newspaper verse and the tiny volumes of vanity publications. Local-color novelists exploited the native scene in regional fragments, bringing to notice the plantations of Louisiana, the mountaineers of Kentucky and Tennessee, the farms of Maine, or the mining camps of the far west, all gilded with the sentimentality of the era. This stream, however thin, did at least, like its contemporary, the earlier realism, recognize the presence of Whitman's simple, democratic man, the American egalitarian note, though with a consequent slackening of dramatic tension. John Burroughs or John Muir, presenting the joys of the out-of-doors in the Catskills or the Rocky Mountains, or Theodore Roosevelt, glorifying the western legend of action and hardihood, reinforced the western saga. In our own day, the nature theme profits greatly by a new scientific precision, the factual replacing the inspirational, and a host of competent twentieth-century books show the poetry that lies in the accurate and the precise, just as a scientific anthropology far surpasses in interest the old romanticism of the natural savage.

But the American tide had changed. The source of that change in literature, however, must be sought in something other than industrial growth or an encroaching population. It lay, instead, in a complexity of intellectual events, not the least of which were scientific in origin, the new geology, the new biology, even the new concepts of history and the obligation of the historian to be impartial and thorough. From this larger cultural shift the term *naturalism* came.

Poets and novelists, it is true, are not obligated to be scientists and philosophers; yet few of them can afford to be indifferent to the intellectual currents of their time. This is a subtle area not always open to a simple clarification. Poetry of any value emerges always from the individual, from a personal energy, seeking expression, coloring whatever passes through its private workshop. Do we need to stress again that literature is neither science, philosophy, history, ethics, or sociology, however involved in similar concerns? It is first of all experience, deeply felt through a given temperament, for better or for worse, which, like flame seeking fuel, consumes books, ideas, theories, popular waves of sentiment, or profounder reflections of men's minds to feed the central drive, the living knowledge of the creator mind. Conformity to any of these other elements, or to conventional expression, is imitation, death to the creative urge, not experience. The Emersonian insistence is valid still, if one would distinguish between those who but echo the books they read, the environment they know, and those who step off afresh in new explorations.

Similarly, the novelist is not merely one who has some theory to exploit, psychological, social, or moral, but one who casts his knowledge into the form of portraying concrete human beings in human situations on the level of individual experience, where all is and must be subject still to a free examination, a fresh reflection on the original chaos of indecision and doubt. The way to kill a novel is to load it with a preconceived thesis, an abstraction, which reduces all its characters to puppets moved about to prove an unreality. Scientist and philosopher generalize particular observations; poet and novelist particularize generalizations, if, indeed, they have generalizations foremost in mind; and thereby the latter come closer to human experience and correct the abstractions of scientist, philosopher, and specialist, insofar as these apply to actual human beings. For these reasons, some Darwin or Freud never wholly explains literature or what happens in literature. Nevertheless, the impact of the thinking of such great figures may immensely stimulate the creative writer to new starts and new insights in his study of the individual human predicament.

What happened was that the younger American writers in the post–Civil War period, seeking a weapon against the prevailing genteelism, found it in the newer scientific outlook and in naturalism, borrowed in part from Europe but given its native transmutation. This term "naturalism," implicit even in an eighteenth-century empiricism, and long before Darwin's bombshell, was given a considerable impetus by Lyell's *Principles of Geology,* which appeared in the early 1830's. This book vastly expanded the time concept of the globe and, like Darwin's later work (1859), stretched men's minds to contemplate long-range natural processes, impersonal in nature, and far antedating man.[1] Naturalism, more specifically applied to literature, arose when Zola and others took over from the new sciences their deterministic implications and explored the possibility of approaching man with similar techniques. The novelist, Zola maintained, "is but a recorder, who is forbidden to judge and to conclude." The naturalist in literature wished to experiment with a new technique, that of approaching human behavior as predetermined by laws mechanical, depersonalized, wholly devoid of concern for man's wishes, however passionate. Such an approach, they speculated, might greatly advance the novel as realistic and trustworthy. It has been said that it was Thomas Hardy who removed the capital *N* from nature; equally probable is it that to Herbert Spencer goes this honor, if we may trust the statements of more than one young American in the 1880's. For to the implacable laws of nature as scientifically conceived he added a kind of system and unity which introduced order where there had been a chaos of meaningless forces.

Thus from foreign models American writers took renewed cour-

---

[1] If one may be pardoned a personal note, it was an ancient greenbacked copy of Lyell's *Principles of Geology* found in a country school in the Mohawk Valley that stirred the writer to a first awareness of the cosmic history and poetry that lay in science.

age to attack the American scene with a new freedom. One must recognize how greatly Darwin, Spencer, the new sciences, eventually the new psychology, conspired in the following decades to whittle down man's romantic pretensions to be the master of events in a universe of complex and impersonal forces. Neither the old nomadic urge nor the romantic "communion with her visible forms" could survive the shock unchanged. No American writer, unless it had been Melville, had clearly anticipated this new, impersonal nature; and even his was a passionate protest, not a modern grimness of acceptance, even though the relevancy of his insights must account in part for a present popularity of *Moby-Dick* in an existentialist Europe.

Under these circumstances—and it should be remembered that a new movement may be less in the nature of an assertion of truth with a capital *T* than a query as to what would happen if we tried this new approach—the young American writer had certain choices: he might linger nostalgically amid older themes and so lose his place (where are Bret Harte and Bayard Taylor today?); he might plunge headlong into new controversies, sacrificing creativity to polemics; or he might, like many modern artists, turn inward to explore his own subjective, even surrealistic, world as the final retreat for the thin-skinned personality in a hostile world or, again, as an exploration of a new source of materials. Or, in the manner of more abiding artists, he might wrestle as best he could with the currents and dilemmas of his own generation, putting out sensitive antennae to catch the hints that flowed to him and to translate them into poem or novel.

The American writer after 1870 was by no means unaware of the foreign currents—Howells absorbing Tolstoi, James savoring Flaubert and Turgenev, the young Norris aping Zola. But each remained faithful to some aspect of the native scene. James in "The Art of Fiction" made much of experience as the base, though not, it is true, in the name of naturalism. His analogies he preferred to draw from the art of the portrait painter: realism coupled with subtle insights, concentration on the skills of execution, an indifference to the popular demands for shallow entertainment, instruction, or conventional didacticism. He liked to free his characters, for his purposes, from the pressures of gross poverty and ignorance and take them from the conscious levels of society where language and manners have attained some sophistication. Howells, surely no convert to naturalism, in his turn stirred younger men to look more sharply at their own environment; men like Norris, Stephen Crane, and Hamlin Garland, who exhibited in their output a compound of American idealism, western scenery, and the ironies of man pitted against impersonal, larger-than-human forces.

Echoes of the new note soon appeared in the young men whom Howells had encouraged. Who does not recall Stephen Crane's ironic little poem:

> A man said to the universe
> "Sir, I exist!"
> "However," replied the universe,
> "The fact has not created in me
> A sense of obligation." [2]

Or the protest of the correspondent in Crane's "The Open Boat":

When it occurs to a man that Nature does not regard him as important, and that she feels she would not maim the universe by disposing of him, he at first wishes to throw bricks at the temple, and he hates deeply the fact that there are no bricks and no temples.[3]

Or, in the same story, "the serenity of nature and the struggles of the individual—nature in the wind, and nature in the vision of men. She did not seem cruel to him then, nor beneficent, nor treacherous, nor wise. But she was indifferent, flatly indifferent." [4] When the

---

[2] Stephen Crane, *Collected Poems*, p. 101.
[3] Crane, "The Open Boat," *Twenty Stories*, p. 231.
[4] *Ibid.*, p. 236.

men who escape drowning feel, at the end of the story, that "they could be interpreters," what they have learned is precisely this flat indifference in nature. This is a far cry from Bryant's "communion" with nature's visible forms, or Emerson's "Nature" as symbol and analogy for the aspirations of spirit.

Yet Crane is never wholly naturalist. Behind the amazing objectivity, for a boy of twenty-two, of *Maggie: A Girl of the Streets* is the give-away of an inscription in an early edition, revealing the American compulsion to better the conditions which determinism has caused:

For it [this book] tries to show that environment is a tremendous thing in the world and frequently shapes lives regardless. If one proves that theory, one makes room in heaven for all sorts of souls, notably an occasional street girl, who are not confidently expected to be there by many excellent people.[5]

The first sentence is naturalistic in tone. The second reveals the protest against the smugness of "many excellent people." Crane's meteoric genius, after all, lay in the reporter's eye and the impressionistic highlighting of a poetic language, given sinew by the new note of grim determinism: "A high cold star on a winter's night is the word he feels that she says to him. Thereafter he knows the pathos of his situation." [6]

Frank Norris went beyond Crane in one respect, at least, in that nature for him is no longer "she," but "it": "relentless, a gigantic engine, a vast power, huge, terrible; a leviathan with a heart of steel, knowing no compunction, no forgiveness, no tolerance; crushing out the human atom with soundless calm." [7] The "boy Zola," as he liked to be called, could, nevertheless, never quite bring himself to the

---

[5] This inscription, which I have not been able to locate elsewhere, is quoted by William M. Gibson in his Introduction to the Rinehart edition of *Stephen Crane: Selected Prose and Poetry,* p. ix.

[6] Crane, "The Open Boat," *Twenty Stories,* p. 232.

[7] Frank Norris, *The Octopus,* p. 124.

objective amorality of Zola's creed; and the overtones are "reforming"
still. Like Jack London's "law of claw and fang," the echo is again
from Herbert Spencer, whom London had picked up one evening
to put himself to sleep, and had instead read until dawn with a
growing inward excitement. The step is not far, then, to Theodore
Dreiser, but one year younger than Norris, whose early *Sister Carrie*
(1900) had actually set Norris off on his trilogy of American life.
Dreiser's self-tutored view of life as merely a matter of chemical-
biological forces, "a damned stinking game," in which the rules are
solely those of a ruthless competition and the temporary victories of
the most ruthless, is likewise a compound of Spencer and of Dreiser's
own private suffering.

The immediate influence of these seminaturalists, however, was
not deep; and the period of 1890 to 1910 saw a new tide of sentimentality which all but drowned the new realists and which was
destined to exasperate a generation nurtured on this feeble pap and
then thrown into the cauldron of World War I. Nothing is so calculated to stir a good man to a hard-boiled realism as the discovery
that sentimentalism is a poor preparation for life's rawer thrusts.
The evidence is in Melville, Crane, or London, as well as in later
writers—but World War I caught a whole generation nurtured on
a thin gruel indeed. Henry James's definitions have been quoted
before, but merit repetition here: realism as "the things we cannot
possibly *not* know, sooner or later, in one way or another," and romanticism as "the things that, with all the facilities in the world, all
the wealth and all the courage and all the wit and all the adventure,
we never *can* directly know." [8] These distinctions a softer America
had to rediscover.

The generation of the 1920's, therefore, had to assert themselves,
insulate themselves against a prevailing smugness and lack of self-
criticism. Malcolm Cowley stated it thus: "Honest writing in this

[8] Henry James, *The American,* p. xvi.

country . . . has almost always been the work of an opposition, chiefly because . . . a man who accepts orthodox judgments is in danger of losing his literary personality." [9] Indirectly, then, a certain isolation would seem to be, in one way or another, the lot of the creative writer. But it is not, or should not be, an end, only perhaps a tool of his freedom to be creative, a price he pays against becoming the pawn of shallower aspirations.

There is not space here to trace the manifestations of this new attitude toward American nature and its consequences in American literature, though samplings will rush to mind: Dreiser or Robinson Jeffers, these two perhaps nearest to naturalism in their belittlement of man's freedom to choose; Sherwood Anderson, brooding over the warped and thwarted careers in little midwestern towns, the backwaters of the original northwest frontier with all its hopes, and, out of the very intensity of his empathy with his victims, stumbling upon a semi-Freudian technique for depicting the grotesques of an inner isolation and solitude; Edgar Lee Masters and Sinclair Lewis in their more positive attacks upon the same no-longer-frontier small towns as sterile, devoid of culture, hostile to the creative spirit; and other lesser writers in the same general direction, driving home the decay of the old American surge westward and the cost in frustration and esthetic barrenness.

Ernest Hemingway comes a trifle later, in his own rugged way another American insister on the old theme of a reliance on the direct experience and a return to nature in the raw. It is as if, in the western tradition, he had to prove himself on the frontiers of a physical testing. Is it a pose, a prolonged adolescence, a frontier inheritance, this admiration for muscle and silent heroics? Like Huck Finn, Hemingway must "light out for the territory," where there is little of civilization; for "I been there before." It is a phenomenon of the American scene that men of action seem too often to shame

[9] Malcolm Cowley, "Naturalism in American Literature," reprinted in *Evolutionary Thought in America*, ed. Stow Persons, p. 330.

the men of contemplation into at least the simulacrum of admiration for action above reflection, the necessity to demonstrate that one is also capable of physical performance.

Hemingway, at any rate, sought always the frontiers of physical experience, in war, bullfighting, big-game hunting in Africa, in men of few words and resolute action—in places, we might almost say, where thinking was at a minimum and speech on the inarticulate levels of a third-rate "western." There is, therefore, an eternal boyishness about Hemingway. Nevertheless, he had his code, his measure of what it was to be a writer. Put down, he said, "what really happened in action; what the actual things were which produced the emotion which you experienced." The great thing, he said, was to "write when there is something that you know; and not before; and not too damned much after. Let those who want to [,] save the world if you can get to see it clear and whole." He was determined, he announced, to write "without tricks and without cheating." [10] "Don't lie to yourself," he has Robert Jordan say in *For Whom the Bell Tolls,* " . . . nor make up literature about it." [11] Thus Maxwell Geismar in his *Writers in Crisis* was able to speak of Hemingway's "total renunciation of all social frameworks . . . [his] acceptance of a profound isolation as a basis for the writer's achievement." [12]

Even the poets, the imagists, groped their way toward a new realism, echoing Whitman's no similes, no borrowed phrases, the rhythms of natural speech. And who more Whitman-like than Carl Sandburg, singing the cities and farmlands of the central basin of America and the natural setting for a Lincoln? Novelists, too, revive the old note of the American scene in its vastness and solitude and subtle appeal. Thomas Wolfe rises to floodtides of polyphonic prose, a southern rhetoric, on the theme.

[10] Ernest Hemingway, quoted in Joseph Warren Beach, *American Fiction, 1920–1940,* pp. 73–74.

[11] *Ibid.,* p. 90.

[12] Maxwell Geismar, *Writers in Crisis,* p. 39.

In *From Death to Morning,* Wolfe writes that the true history of America runs

> back through poverty, and hardship, through solitude and loneliness and death and unspeakable courage, into the wilderness. For it is the wilderness that is the mother of that nation: it was in the wilderness that the strange and lonely people who have not yet spoken . . . first knew themselves. . . . The real history . . . is a history of solitude, of the wilderness, and of the eternal earth . . . the immense and terrible earth that makes no answer.[13]

This is the old note, the Whitmanesque note, American history expounded in terms of a mystic meaning, with a believer's license to persuade the emotions; whether it be historical truth or not, it is, like Whitman's lines, an attempt to give the "long dumb voices" their voice.

Proper names, too, as for Whitman, ring for Wolfe like trumpet calls to celebrate the length and breadth of our land, "imperial names," names which reduce the Tiber and the Thames to the rivulets which they are. Wolfe has one passage of nearly ten pages of American names alone, each one presumably rich with the connotations of pride and folk appeal. Less expansively, Hemingway likewise, though for a different reason, in *Farewell to Arms* puts mere place names above "noble words" as evokers of past experience, the strange, mixed emotions of men remembering the shared experience of another more literal battle front.

And who does not recall Wolfe's haunting evocation of trains by night, passing over the greatness of the land, sliding into little towns, striding through fields and across rivers, the huge trains of America and the gigantic engines? The quotation is from *Of Time and the River.*

> Then the train slides by the darkened vacant-looking little station and for a moment one had a glimpse of the town's chief square and business

---

[13] Thomas Wolfe, *From Death to Morning,* pp. 203–204.

center. And as he sees it he is filled again with the same feeling of loneliness, instant familiarity, and departure. . . . A moment's vision of a dusty
little street . . . a silent little square, and then the darkness of the earth
again. . . . The new standards of the five-bulbed lamps cast down implacably upon those cataleptic pavements the cataleptic silence of their
hard white light. . . . Then the train, running always with its smooth,
powerful, almost noiseless movement, has left the station and the square
behind it . . . and there is nothing but huge and secret night before us,
the lonely, everlasting earth.[14]

In Faulkner, too, naturalism or any other "ism" is forgotten in the
deeper, essentially American note of nostalgia for the lost frontier,
the mystique of the frontier as a missed opportunity, a forfeited
Eden. Perhaps nothing better than the passage quoted below from
Faulkner's "The Bear" illustrates how in his own apartness he man-
ages to give vitality to what is essentially a folklore concept. This is
hardly a new theme, and an occasional reader may recall Colonel
Woodburn of William Dean Howells' *A Hazard of New Fortunes*
(1890), who will be found to preach an almost identical sentiment,
though in far less impassioned language.

In that long short-story, "The Bear," a boy has been initiated, step
by step, into the annual ritual of hunting Old Ben the bear, until,
as a man, he has come to elicit from the event a profound meaning,
so profound that he voluntarily relinquishes his claim to his paternal
inheritance, and deeds over the land to his cousin McCaslin Edmonds. His reason for doing this is a strange mixture of mysticism
about the American past and the shock of discovering within the
family history the blots of miscegenation and exploitation. The original Indian inhabitants, Ike McCaslin argues, had no right to sell or
to deed the land in the first place; and white sale and deed are thus
equally invalid. God himself, Ike reasons, enabled Europeans to discover the New World as a second chance at redemption from Eu-

---

14 Wolfe, *Of Time and the River*, pp. 31–35 *passim*.

rope's accumulated sins; now this new Eden has been despoiled, and man again driven forth from it for his crimes.

The passages which communicate this outpouring of feeling are, such is the Faulknerian manner, far too long to quote *in toto,* but an excerpt or two will illustrate. Faulkner, like Wolfe, suffers from a kind of compulsiveness of language which renders quotation awkward. The speaker is Ike McCaslin, now in his young manhood. The egg reference is, of course, to the story of Columbus. The subject is Europe's past and America's lost paradise:

Men . . . snarled . . . in the old world's worthless twilight over the old world's gnawed bones, blasphemous in His name until He used a simple egg to discover to them a new world where a nation of people could be founded in humility and pity and sufferance and pride of one to another. . . . from that old world's corrupt and worthless twilight as though in sailfuls of the old world's tainted wind which drove the ships. . . .

and, continuing the theme pages later:

Until He said . . . *This Is Enough* and looked . . . upon this land this South for which He had done so much with woods for game and streams for fish and deep rich soil for seed and lush springs to sprout it and long summers to mature it and serene falls to harvest it and short mild winters for men and animals and saw no hope anywhere and looked beyond it where hope should have been, where to East North and West lay illimitable that whole hopeful continent dedicated as a refuge and sanctuary of liberty and freedom from what you called the old world's worthless evening . . . [etc.] [15]

The pages which follow constitute a prolonged review of the abuses heaped upon this once hopeful land, south and north, a land where "apparently they can learn nothing save through suffering, remember nothing save when underlined in blood";[16] and, after further pages which review the sad tale of the South, white and black,

[15] William Faulkner, "The Bear," *Go Down, Moses,* pp. 258–259, 283.
[16] *Ibid.,* p. 286.

"Apparently there is a wisdom beyond even that learned through suffering necessary for a man to distinguish between liberty and license," [17] for the crime is that generals and politicians go to war not for freedom but to preserve a status quo and to better the lot of their own private group. And all these breathless, rarely punctuated sentences (the style is contagious) are Ike's justification for his relinquishment of his claim to the land, and his turning in symbolic fashion to carpentering, not at all because he fancies himself a kind of Christ, but simply because he is a man making a gesture that he must make.

How shall one read this whole story if not as one more appeal to the theme of the frontier as a lost opportunity, a last chance for man to create a new Eden of freedom and justice? This knowledge the boy garnered not from books but from the annual hunt, which to the older men who took him along was fun, a vacation, an escape from town, but which to the boy, growing to see the passing of the event, becomes much more, a glimpse into the profound wisdom of elemental nature. And this he learned, too, from Old Ben, the bear, and from Sam Fathers, half-Indian, half-Negro, with whom this instinctive, elemental knowledge must die except as Ike may grasp it and retain it.

What Ike has learned, then, is something antedating cities and civilizations and formalized religions, something akin to Thoreau's knowledge that man lives within nature, and must not abuse his side of the equation. Like the balance within the Indian's respect for beast and country, like the frontiersman's knowledge, like Hemingway's art, this wisdom is to be drawn from the original, the elemental experience; and in no sense is it a bookish or an institutionalized tradition. The boy is a belated Natty Bumppo once more, belated because only as it is passing does he glimpse a simple rightness in the forest pattern and in the hunters' respect for the old bear. As

[17] *Ibid.*, p. 289.

something died with Leatherstocking on the prairie, facing the western sun, so something died for Ike with the death of the old bear, and the death of Sam Fathers, the old guide, and with the sale of the forest to a progressive, enterprising lumber company. That knowledge, that wisdom, may be lost forever, for as McCaslin Edmonds says sadly to Ike: "It took you fourteen years to reach this point. How long then? How long?"

Mr. R. W. B. Lewis, in a perceptive article on Faulkner in the *Kenyon Review,* argued that "The Bear" is the one tale in which Faulkner tips the scale of the tensions between the creative and the destructive in favor of nature as a source of creative values. I am forced, therefore, to quote here from Professor Lewis, since he has put into two sentences what I should have hesitated to phrase so sharply for fear of riding my thesis too hard:

> The central poetic insight [says Lewis] . . . which Faulkner has shared with Mark Twain and many another American writer is . . . an insight into the fertile and ambiguous possibility of moral freedom in the new world. . . . The frontier, as Turner and Constance Rourke were the first to make clear, was the major physical source of this uniquely American idea; the idea . . . of a new, unspoiled area in which a genuine and radical moral freedom could once again be exercised.[18]

Assuming these two sentences to be defensible, they imply, as these pages have attempted to do, that there is a discoverable and a genuine thread of frontier impact running through all American literature, applying to each in its way—Cooper, Emerson, Thoreau, Hawthorne, Melville, Whitman, or, here, Wolfe and Faulkner. The implications of that impact, furthermore, reach to touch an independence of reflection and a search for an original footing far deeper than the political alone.

Naturalism, as a brief literary movement, would seem in compari-

[18] R. W. B. Lewis, "The Hero in the New World: William Faulkner's 'The Bear'," *Kenyon Review,* 13 (Autumn, 1951), 641–660.

son a relatively superficial phenomenon, or, better yet, one to be viewed as a needed protest against a prevailing romanticism, an acceptance of the responsibilities of a maturing fiction. Behind the old romantic novel there had not been much critical apparatus; there had been much concession to popular mores and popular optimism, with a consequent Victorian evasion of the franker and the more brutal. Whitman attempted the greater frankness in the name of his transcendental egalitarianism; but his effort was met largely with silence. The harsher notes from Zola and Spencer were needed if the American creative impulse were to free itself from a growing unreality within a modern world. The youthful underlining of the deterministic note would give way in time to the older American optimism; but the impact of the experiment would remain to show itself in indirect ways on all future American work. Fiction lives, as James said, by experiment, by new insights, by new efforts to see life more clearly and to render it plausibly and convincingly. Yet, in this choice between what we cannot *not* know, sooner or later, and what we can *never* know, for all our wealth or wishing, the American writer would not lose sight of the native symbols for the pragmatic experience. Even the poets would maintain the old theme in fresher forms.

xiv. How Clean the Sun

> *The trouble of the mind*
> *Is a residue, a land, a rain, a warmth.*[1]
>
> —Wallace Stevens

IN PREVIOUS PAGES we have touched upon the American writer's effort to grasp the significance of his countrymen's experience on the geographical frontiers, and to exploit that experience as symbol and metaphor for a national aspiration and a native literature. In a twentieth century, when a literal frontier is no longer available, and few, if any, poets would wish to return to those simpler modes, it is but fair to ask what may be the fate of this central theme.

One of our observations would be, indeed, that few of our major poets today concern themselves with the nationalistic note. None of the three or four mentioned below, for example, is interested in any degree in the frontier legend as such, nor with the American self-boast on that once great migration. Poets today are lonelier souls, renouncing the role of spokesmen for a nation, accepting as inevita-

---

[1] From Wallace Stevens, "How Now, O Brightener," *Opus Posthumous,* p. 97.

ble a certain remoteness from the general reader, and even, in our far-flung land, from one another.

As we turn to three major voices, now unhappily silent, we find that one of them, Robert Frost, does, indeed, contain much to link him with the old New England note, and did achieve a position something analogous to that of a national poet laureate. But his link is with a transcendentalist independency, and he moves from the heart of New England outward to his cosmic hints. The other two, Robinson Jeffers and Wallace Stevens, are marked by their withdrawal from the central stream; yet they serve admirably as a kind of appropriate climax to our whole study, each presenting nature as clean and austere, stripped of man's prime illusions, and contemplated in almost nonhuman terms. Jeffers ends the long trajectory from Atlantic to Pacific, and pauses on the last headlands to reject man's intrusion on the vast geologic scheme of things; whereas Wallace Stevens, highly urban, probes ever deeper to catch nature's very lineaments in and of themselves, stripped of man's incurable fictions. All three of these poets show deeply ingrained habits of self-sufficiency; all refuse to compromise with the prejudices of the market place, being equally indifferent to party or politics. All three, it may be asserted, are American, in the sense that they are not to be easily duplicated elsewhere.

Were we to dwell at any length on the Hawthornesque theme of solitude, we should have to consider a fourth figure, Edwin Arlington Robinson. Who more surely has echoed Hawthorne's profound sense of human solitude? If Robert Frost seems a twentieth-century Thoreau in his earthy shrewdness and dry whimsy, Robinson more than any other modern figure carries the mark of Hawthorne. Whether it be Mr. Flood, drinking his toast to himself in the lonely night on a hillside above the town, or *Matthias at the Door,* discovering in the suicides of his closest friend and his wife his own mortal weakness and so forging wisdom from defeat, or the philosophic strains of *The Man Against the Sky,* with its refrain of

"Mostly alone he goes," Robinson's, like Hawthorne's, is a minimal transcendentalism, skeptical, solitary, profoundly aware of the ambiguities that forever link self-reliance and solitude. Robinson's central theme is not nature, but human nature; and his occasional references to the setting of nature are likely to be signals for a return to the fireside. Solitude is his theme, but not that of the raw frontier.

I

Robert Frost has so long been the accepted poet of America that one should be on guard against the superficial measures of popularity. His is, on the surface, Emily Dickinson's "The simple news that nature told," the obvious rural settings, the simple folk tied to the land, the excursions into field and forest; he merits a deeper look.

Frost is an elusive poet, possessing a true Yankee suspicion of premature absolutes, and preferring to hide layer behind layer of meaning; but it does not take long to discover in his poems the immediacy of nature's presence. Earth for him is man's home, his habitation, the nurse of his strength, and the source of all that is self-discovery. From one of the first of his poems, "Into My Own," to the eerie dialogue of mist and smoke in one of his last, the title poem of his *In the Clearing,* Frost makes use of the woods as holding in their darkness secrets which man never quite possesses. In "Into My Own," the dark trees are extended in imagination "unto the edge of doom," and the youth would plunge into them beyond human tracks, to be found by those who follow to seek him "only more sure of all I thought was true." [2] The older man is not so confident of his own wisdom, if more aware of the sure foundations of his habitation. In the clearing, just enough

> To push the woods back from around the house
> And part them in the middle with a path,

[2] Robert Frost, "Into My Own," *Complete Poems of Robert Frost,* p. 5.

a tiny cabin holds sleeping human beings who hardly know where they are. Why do they not ask the Indians? say mist and smoke; why not their philosophers and scientists, hoping to find truth in the accumulation of data? They have done so; yet they huddle in the tiny cabin still for warmth, for

> Than smoke and mist who better can appraise
> The kindred spirit of an inner haze.[3]

The ocean, too, can symbolize the endless query of man, as in "Neither Out Far Nor In Deep," in which poem the folk stand on the shore and wonder, though they can see neither out far nor in deep,

> But when was that ever a bar
> To any watch they keep?[4]

A poem that at first reading may seem innocuously simple turns out on further examination to carry the same overtones of man's ultimate dependence on what he can never quite subdue. Take, for example, "It Bids Pretty Fair":

> The play seems out for an almost infinite run.
> Don't mind a little thing like the actors fighting.
> The only thing I worry about is the sun.
> We'll be all right if nothing goes wrong with the lighting.[5]

One word only does not fit into the overt statement—the word *sun*. Suddenly the whole shifts to man's play as anthropoid, both ends of the plot lost in darkness. Man appears pretty secure on his globe, despite his warring; but what if the sun go out—the lighting? With wry irony, Frost reminds little man of his eternal dependence on nature's silent machinery. The real play, as Frost has said elsewhere, is "for keeps." It is not necessary to seek for symbolism or "message."

---

[3] Frost, "A Cabin in the Clearing," from *In the Clearing*, pp. 16–18.
[4] Frost, "Neither Out Far Nor In Deep," *Complete Poems*, p. 394.
[5] Frost, "It Bids Pretty Fair," *ibid.*, p. 555.

The poem is a simple statement of fact, neither pessimistic nor optimistic, humorous, deadly serious, and rooted in fact. Such is Frost, at his most characteristic, his best, even his simplest.

Said Emerson in *Nature,* "It seems as if the day was not wholly profane in which we have given heed to some natural object." Such is Frost's observation in a casual poem like "Dust of Snow."

> The way a crow
> Shook down on me
> The dust of snow
> From a hemlock tree
>
> Has given my heart
> A change of mood
> And saved some part
> Of a day I had rued.[6]

So simple a poem is no work of a momentary impulse but of a long immersion in the solitudes of a rural habitat, a participation in nature's diurnal round. It contains no overstatement, no straining for effect, no forced symbolism. It is, indeed, within the New England laconic tradition, sparing, modest, individual.

Poem after poem might be brought forward to illustrate Frost's dependence on nature for his subject matter and factual base. The title poem of his *West-Running Brook* has the familiar westward theme in a personal form—the lone brook in New England that persists, like Thoreau's walking, in turning west when all else seeks the Atlantic, yet which flows "*with* us," in a "backward motion [i.e., in the white wave of a ripple] toward the source." [7] In "The Wood-Pile," in which the labor of man, neatly stacked in the depths

---

[6] Frost, "Dust of Snow," *ibid.*, p. 270.
[7] Frost, "West-Running Brook," *ibid.*, p. 329.

of the woods, is forgotten and slowly returns to earth, the meaning
is in the last lines:

> To warm the frozen swamp as best it could
> With the slow smokeless burning of decay.[8]

Man's labors never succeed in denying this natural base, these
permanent forces. In "Range-Finding" a bullet cuts a cobweb and
a flower in a pasture. But the bird still seeks its young, the butterfly
its flower, and the spider, running out when the dew is shaken from
its web, finding nothing, withdraws to wait again. Nothing has
really happened to shake nature. Again, in "A Brook in the City,"
the brook that once ran clearly by a farmhouse is now forced under-
ground into the sewer and the "meadow grass cemented down," but

> How . . . dispose of an immortal force
> No longer needed? [9]

Perhaps from this denial the city's restlessness in work and sleep
arises.

Frost's awareness of the folk of New England is as deep as Haw-
thorne's or Robinson's. Picture after picture admits the loneliness
of remote farms and small dwellings apart. They err who think
Frost conventionally comforting. He knows the cold whiteness of
Melville's white snows, the stars, in the phrase of an early poem,
"Stars,"

> Like some snow-white
> Minerva's snow-white marble eyes
> Without the gift of sight. [10]

In "An Old Man's Winter Night," the unsparing "Out, Out—," or
"The Hill Wife," Frost touches the ultimate in isolation and stoic
acceptance of what must be.

---

[8] Frost, "The Wood-Pile," *ibid.*, p. 126.
[9] Frost, "A Brook in the City," *ibid.*, p. 285.
[10] Frost, "Stars," *ibid.*, p. 12.

In these "samples," as Frost has called his poems, he is, in his own term, the "synecdochist," in whom the parts stand for the whole. That whole he does not attempt to pin down, accepting, perhaps, Thoreau's definition of religion, "that which is not spoken." For Frost is as serenely indifferent to any final credo as is Emerson or Thoreau—the minimal transcendentalist again, like Robinson, though a more confident one. Frost has never pushed his talent to the vatic, the prophetical. He is content to dwell on his planet and accept his lot as poet-sampler, for whom "no acquirement is on assignment, or even self-assignment." [11] It is this casual refusal to be caught in premature commitments that acts as an irritant on certain of his critics. The nearest he has come, perhaps, to a personal declaration is in a brief passage in his *Masque of Mercy*, in which his own voice seems to penetrate the disguise of the Keeper, turning finally from his good-humored comments on the side to this statement:

> When a great tide of argument sweeps in
> My small fresh water spring gets drowned of course.
> But when the brine goes back as go it must
> I can count on my source to spring again
> Not even brackish from its salt experience.
> No true source can be poisoned. [12]

This is the true Emersonian vein, the self-reliance of the one who finds his inner source in the original connotation of the fresh-water spring. It is said that American lecturers abroad find it not easy to present Frost to foreign audiences. If this be true, it may be that Frost is too wholly New England in his spare speech and manner, the restraint on his admissions, the remoteness from familiar cultural expectations of the European listener. Frost belongs, finally, not to the American frontier, but to the New England inheritance on the frontiers of thought, asking of his country only "originality

[11] Frost, "The Figure a Poem Makes," *ibid.*, p. viii.
[12] Frost, *Masque of Mercy, ibid.*, p. 633.

and initiative." He belongs to no school or movement. He belongs
to us all.

II

Robinson Jeffers likewise forces his own category. He, too, is an
original. Seeing life in what is perhaps now somewhat dated geologic
fashion, the grim geologic determinism of an earlier view that dooms
the globe to a final freezing in the sun's waning or a burning in its
final flare, Jeffers paints man on that stage as petty indeed, existing
in concern for his own comfort and lust and illusion and in a kind of
wilful blindness to the austere, self-sufficient beauty about him.

Jeffers was the product of and the poet of the Californian coast,
and drew his stark images from its granite cliffs and seared hills, or
from the hawk's swift plunge upon its victims. Here, said Jeffers in
an earlier period, he found a few folk living "amid magnificent
unspoiled scenery . . . Here was life purged of its ephemeral accretions. Men were riding after cattle, or plowing the headland, hov-
ered by white seagulls, as they have done for thousands of years." [13]
And here, in his long, powerful, free verse lines, Jeffers celebrated
the violence and the overpowering beauty of the vast, impersonal
reality of a nature which, as Thoreau had already noted, had long
ago taken its resolutions and its form without consulting man's
little desires. And if Jeffers has dwelt often in his longer poems
on the violence of incest and murder, it is that by such means he
symbolizes man's incurable passion for viewing his universe in terms
of his own introverted wishes and lusts, justifying his behavior or
beliefs simply on the ground that they are his. Nature, unlike human
beings, is in Jeffers always austere, pure, passionless even in storm.
How, he asks in a shorter poem, "Gale in April," has man managed
to survive these implacable forces:

[13] Robinson Jeffers, *The Selected Poetry of Robinson Jeffers,* pp. xv–xvi.

Intense and terrible beauty, how has our race with the
    frail naked nerves,
So little a craft swum down from its far launching?
Why now, only because the northwest blows and the headed
    grass billows,
Great seas jagging the west and on the granite
Blanching, the vessel is brimmed, this dancing play of the
    world is too much passion.
A gale in April so overfilling the spirit,
Though his ribs were thick as the earth's, arches of mountain,
    how shall one dare to live,
Though his blood were like the earth's rivers and his
    flesh iron,
How shall one dare to live? One is born strong, how do
    the weak endure it? [14]

Here is neither the old romantic nature of Wordsworth or the
transcendentalist, nor yet the ironic protest of a Crane or Norris.
This seeks beauty in acceptance, not in denial of the harsh or the
ugly. One of his most beautiful poems, "Night," combines the beauty
and the acceptance. It begins with the image of night coming down
over the coastal hills to the western ocean; Night, "the splendor
without rays, the shining of shadow,/ Peace-bringer." Night is the
mother of all shining, all light, from the tiniest glowworm or the
lamp in the midnight tower to the greatest of all stars, "out of grasp
of the mind enormous," yet each an ephemeral flame destined to
burn out with time in a return to the universal mother, Night. For
Night is at once the primal memory and the prophecy of what is to
come. The poem ends, therefore, upon a modern query which
emerges from this contemplation of the cosmic mother:

Have men's minds changed,
Or the rock hidden in the deep waters of the soul
Broken the surface? A few centuries
Gone by, was none dared not to people

[14] Jeffers, "Gale in April," *Roan Stallion, Tamar, and Other Poems*, p. 170.

> The darkness beyond the stars with harps and habitations.
> But now, dear is the truth. Life is grown sweeter
>   and lonelier,
> And death is no evil. [15]

On the last western shore of the New World America, a western poet has framed beauty not out of the conquest of a frontier but out of an austere denial of man's fondest imaginings upon himself.

But Jeffers has not utterly denied man either place or meaning; he has simply refused to separate him from the faceless nature in which he has his being. Within that setting man, too, may be ennobled. Looking out through the fog, for example, the poet glimpses six boats creeping, "patient and cautious . . . following the cliff for guidance," and again disappearing in the mist; and he reflects that nothing is nobler than this kind of unseen glimpse of men going seriously about their business:

> The flight of the planets is nothing nobler; all the arts
>   lose virtue
> Against the essential reality
> Of creatures going about their business among the equally
> Earnest elements of nature. [16]

It must be admitted, however, that despite an occasional concession of this sort, man, to Jeffers, appears to be among the least appealing of natural phenomena. Thus he can become the prophet of disaster. How foreknowing, for example, away back in 1925, this comment from his poem on Science:

> Man, introverted man . . .
> Now he's bred knives on nature turns them also inward: they
>   have thirsty points though.
> His mind forebodes his own destruction. [17]

---

[15] Jeffers, "Night," *Selected Poetry*, p. 160.
[16] Jeffers, "Boats in the Fog," *ibid.*, p. 163.
[17] Jeffers, "Science," *Roan Stallion*, p. 101.

Or in his "Apology for Bad Dreams," in 1926, how foreboding; for
here he argues that it is better for man to invent cruel dreams, to
acknowledge cruelty in the world and to imagine victims, lest he
turn upon his fellowmen in lust and hatred, making holocausts of
real victims. Nor is America exempt from the common lot, for, as it
"settles in the mold of its vulgarity, heavily thickening to empire,"
the consolation is that "meteors are not needed less than mountains:
shine, perishing republic"; and the advice is

> For my children, I would have them keep their distance
>   from the thickening center; corruption
> Never has been compulsory, when the cities lie at the
>   monster's feet there are left the mountains.[18]

Beauty, then, must be wrested from the natural fact, the destruction and the violence, and the contemplation of the harsh spirit of the
hawk. Jeffers put his meaning in a powerfully dramatic poem, "Fire
on the Hills":

> The deer were bounding like blown leaves
> Under the smoke in front of the roaring wave of the brush-fire;
> I thought of the smaller lives that were caught.
> Beauty is not always lovely; the fire was beautiful,
>   the terror
> Of the deer was beautiful; and when I returned
> Down the black slopes after the fire had gone by, an eagle
> Was perched on the jag of a burnt pine,
> Insolent and gorged, cloaked in the folded storms of his
>   shoulders.
> He had come from far off for the good hunting
> With fire for his beater to drive the game; the sky
>   was merciless
> Blue, and the hills merciless black,
> The sombre-feathered great bird sleepily merciless between them.
> I thought, painfully, but the whole mind,

[18] Jeffers, "Shine, Perishing Republic," *ibid.,* p. 95.

The destruction that brings an eagle from heaven is better
   than mercy.[19]

Robinson Jeffers was truly a poet of his own land, clinging in a
modern century to the solitudes of nature and fashioning his vision
out of the austere elements of geography and geology and the relentless working of natural forces. No Thoreau, rebuking his neighbors from a nearby cabin on a pond, but a grimmer, modern man,
he turned his back on human folly, or, placing it in perspective
within the total power and turbulence of nature, found in the contemplation a cleansing impersonality and permanence. Traces of a
frontier stoicism there are, as there is flight from the cities, and even
a transcendentalist search in nature for values by which to live.
Thinking with "the whole mind," and painfully, he finds something
better than mercy, namely, nature's steady procession of life and
death, and death and life, and the final return to the primal night.
Even the word "noble," echo of romanticism, he can attach to this
whole, last, hard-won concession to the pull of nature, as in the
following little poem which may be said almost to summarize
Jeffers:

Life From the Lifeless

Spirits and illusions have died,
The naked mind lives
In the beauty of inanimate things.

Flowers wither, grass fades, trees wilt,
The forest is burnt;
The rock is not burnt.

The deer starve, the winter birds
Die on their twigs and lie
In the blue dawns in the snow.

[19] Jeffers, "Fire in the Hills," *Selected Poetry,* p. 359.

> Men suffer want and become
> Curiously ignoble; as prosperity
> Made them curiously vile.
>
> But look how noble the world is,
> The lonely flowing waters, the secret-
> Keeping stones, the flowing sky. [20]

Almost in Robinson Jeffers is nature abstracted from human passion and the human concept of suffering or of delight—almost, but not quite. That final step in American poetry was left for a poet not yet fully comprehended, Wallace Stevens, whose earlier flamboyance has obscured for many the later austerity which more than matches that of Robinson Jeffers without the overtones of pain and rejection.

III

Wallace Stevens, urbanite, easterner, graduate in law, a vice-president of an insurance company, might seem with difficulty to be assimilable to the great stream of American nature poetry. There is no evidence that he possessed any interest in the frontier legend as such or in the lofty landscapes of the west. His early poems reflect the impact of the lush tropical vegetation of the Caribbean islands, as they show also his deep interest in the French symbolists and in French painting. Yet in time, increasingly aloof from literary company, a solitary worker in moments snatched from the life of a businessman, he became an original figure, paring his work of its early romanticism, pursuing his poetic researches into the very nature of experience itself. His major publication came late in life, and its difficulties have prevented his having any large audience.

Yet it can be said that, albeit an expressed enemy of the loosely transcendental, he clearly links the explorations of Emerson or Whitman with a twentieth-century mind. "He . . . distrusted," says Samuel French Morse in an Introduction to the *Opus Posthumous*, "any

---

[20] Jeffers, "Life From the Lifeless," *ibid.,* p. 564.

system of thought which discredited the particulars of experience." [21] "The right to know/ And the right to be are one," said Stevens; and again, "The right/ To know established as the right to be." [22] Like Thoreau, he must be "drenched in reality." "The imagination," said Stevens, "loses vitality as it ceases to adhere to what is real." [23] The pleasure of the poet, he wrote—and it might be the voice of Emerson—"is a pleasure of agreement with the radiant and productive world in which he lives." [24] Emersonian, too, is his "The spirit comes from the body of the world." [25] Like Whitman, he concludes, "The great poems of heaven and hell have been written and the great poem of the earth remains to be written." [26]

Central to Wallace Stevens is his concern with the relationship that binds reality (which may here be defined as what *is, before* our minds begin to distort it) and imagination (which may here be defined as what our minds do to reality, either to distort or to clarify). For reality and imagination must work as equals, and the purpose of a poetic metaphor is to achieve a momentary flash of wholeness, order, completeness. Our minds, so Stevens argues, touch nothing without refashioning, embellishing, and so in varying degrees distorting, falsifying. The poet's function, then, far from being the Platonic one of seeking the unseen beyond man's reach is actually that of recovering what *is*, the reality, from man's incurable distortions. Imagination is therefore not to be banished with the poet but to become the tool of clarification. Poetry, in short, "an interdependence of the imagination and reality as equals," [27] is, as in a

[21] Wallace Stevens, *Opus Posthumous,* p. xxxii.

[22] Stevens, "The Sail of Ulysses," *ibid.,* pp. 101, 102.

[23] Stevens, "The Noble Rider and the Sound of Words," *The Necessary Angel,* p. 6.

[24] Stevens, "The Figure of the Youth as Virile Poet," *ibid.,* p. 57.

[25] Stevens, "Looking Across the Fields . . .," *Collected Poems of Wallace Stevens,* p. 519.

[26] Stevens, "Imagination as Value," *The Necessary Angel,* p. 142.

[27] Stevens, "The Noble Rider," *ibid.,* p. 27.

poem on the angel of reality, "the necessary angel of earth,/ Since, in my sight, you see the earth again." [28]

Stevens, as may be surmised, puts a heavy demand upon the reader, and the demand is, again, a kind of thinking with "the whole mind," a kind of cleansing of one's thinking of self and self's illusions. The poet must recover reality for us, and restore to us its true lineaments and savor. The base, the starting point, then, must be earth, the sensory contact with earth, not with "ideas." His task, indeed, is to help us distinguish between what Stevens has called philosophic truth and poetic truth, between logical truth and empirical truth. For it is the poet who, in Stevens' terms, ceases to be metaphysician and becomes the empiricist; and in this austere world of rectitude of vision the philosopher is no less alien than the reformer, political or social or moral. We live today, said Stevens (who died in 1955), "in an intricacy of new and local mythologies, political, economic, poetic, which are asserted with an ever-enlarging incoherence. This is accompanied by the absence of any authority except force, operative or imminent." [29] Reality, therefore, is not in externals alone, but includes the life that is lived in an empiric world. Things seen can become things not-seen, Stevens seems to say, whether through false memory, myth, poetry, or philosophy; yet all the labors of exhortation and threat would seem to indicate the difficulty of reversing the process and wresting reality out of the not-seen. The poet's task is to begin with and to restore the clarity of things seen. "The most beautiful thing in the world is, of course, the world itself. This is so not only logically but categorically." [30]

Helpful to an understanding of this poet would be a glimpse of the man at work. Stevens is no ordinary and no easy poet, and his poems, even after repeated readings, may baffle. But no attentive

[28] Stevens, "Angel Surrounded by Paysans," *Collected Poems,* p. 496.
[29] Stevens, "The Noble Rider," *The Necessary Angel,* p. 17.
[30] Stevens, *Opus Posthumous,* p. 167.

reader can fail to see how persistently he returns to contact with earth
and sun and stars, the visual, sensual impressions out of which poetry
is to be made. Sun, earth, day, rock, green vegetation, winter, wind
represent earth's existence, the real, what *is*, quite apart from and
untainted by man's retouching imagination and self-reference of
each to himself; whereas moon, air, night, blue, and musical instru-
ments (the "blue guitar") often represent creative imagination, at
work embellishing what is. But it is always perception to which
the mind must turn as the foundation of its reflection. Surrealism,
symbolism for its own sake, Stevens has little use for. "To make a
clam play an accordian is to invent, not to discover."

In a longer poem, "Credences of Summer," the poet begins with
a statement that midsummer is a good time for reflection because
"the mind lays by its troubles and considers." Then comes this
stanza, on which I shall offer a minimum of explication:

> Postpone the anatomy of summer, as
> The physical pine, the metaphysical pine.
> Let's see the very thing and nothing else.
> Let's see it with the hottest fire of sight.
> Burn everything not part of it to ash.
>
> Trace the gold sun about the whitened sky
> Without evasion by a single metaphor.
> Look at it in its essential barrenness
> And say, this is the centre that I seek.[31]

That is, let us postpone analysis of what the difference may be between the actual pine and the pine metaphysically considered. Let
us, instead, concentrate with all we have on the thing itself, to see
"it" alone, discarding every imaginative and imagined addition to
what "it is." The sun, for example, must be seen without the use of
a single metaphor (recall Whitman's resolve to use no similes), must
be seen as "sun" only (compare Thoreau's "This *is*, and no mis-

[31] Stevens, "Credences of Summer," *Collected Poems*, p. 373.

take"), and not as man reflecting and analogizing on what sun may symbolize for him. It is a rejection of the accretions of the metaphysical past more rigorous, because much more specific, than anything in Emerson.

With such a sampling in mind of the method of Stevens, we may approach other passages with more confidence. In his "Notes Toward a Supreme Fiction," Stevens rejects the possibility that natural objects exist only in our inventing minds. No, away with this metaphysical divertisement; nature is there, given, existing, whatever its reality. The whole problem is to grasp its reality without inventing.

> How clean the sun when seen in its idea,
> Washed in the remotest cleanliness of a heaven
> That has expelled us and our images. . . .
>
> There is a project for the sun. The sun
> Must bear no name, gold flourisher, but be
> In the difficulty of what it is to be. [32]

Or let us take the clouds as a further example:

> The first idea was not to shape the clouds
> In imitation. The clouds preceded us. . . .
> We are the mimics. Clouds are pedagogues.
> The air is not a mirror but bare board. [33]

In other words, the clouds taught us to make comparisons through the use of our fanciful inventions; but clouds are not the fanciful shapes we see, nor does the air reflect us; it simply is, a bare "is" on which we write what fancies we will. Or read again from the same poem, most central for Stevens:

> As when the sun comes rising, when the sea
> Clears deeply, when the moon hangs on the wall
> Of heaven-haven. These are not things transformed.

[32] Stevens, "Notes Toward a Supreme Fiction," *ibid.*, p. 381.
[33] *Ibid.*, p. 383.

> Yet we are shaken by them as if they were.
> We reason about them with a later reason. [34]

Sun and moon, in short, are not the things our imaginings make
of them; they are what their first impact was, when they first as-
saulted our purer senses as yet untainted by question and association;
the rest is additive, the expanding of our images until we are shaken
by our own fancies, like a child frightened by his own storytelling.
Must we fictionize? The moon, as moon, moves us more than any
stale legend of Diana, the moon huntress, if we but see it as the
poet sees it, not through our fictions.

We come, thus, to hate outworn fictions and all discarded images
from the past, the romantic clichés of another day. But (as Thoreau
might also have said), "The freshness of the night has been fresh
a long time." So the poet reflects in a poem with the quaint title of
"The Man on the Dump," the refuse heap of discarded images,
glittering still in the moonlight—but, having learned to see

> As a man (not like an image of a man),
> You see the moon rise in the empty sky. [35]

we can no longer spoil the night's freshness with images of our own.

Stevens was fond of the musical analogy. In "Sad Strains of a
Gay Waltz," his thesis is that the once-gay waltz tune, its subtleties
now faded and lost in a changing world, is "no longer a mode of
desire." [36] So it becomes sad. But "some harmonious skeptic soon in
a skeptical music" will unite men and times again in a new tune,
and music will again have motion and the shadows of desire. The
artist discards, the artist creates anew from the reality behind all.
In the better-known "The Man with the Blue Guitar," [37] Stevens
symbolizes the artist composing his tune on things as they seem, yet

---

[34] *Ibid.*, pp. 398–399.
[35] Stevens, "The Man on the Dump," *Collected Poems*, p. 202.
[36] Stevens, "Sad Strains," *ibid.*, p. 121.
[37] Stevens, "The Man with the Blue Guitar," *ibid.*, p. 165.

to do so, being obliged to look about him at what *is*, and to include man in his tune. The best we can ask is that we be not forever committed to a single tune; for even if the tune grow stale, the strings are always fresh, awaiting the new touch of creation.

Stevens is not writing himself out of poetry, but returning, as it were, to "the many things that seem to be poetry without any intervention on our part, as, for example, the blue sky." [38] Poetry is itself a reality, not bringing into the world, but showing the actual through sensibilities more acute than our own.

A look at a few briefer poems, Stevens' longer poems being beyond the scope of this modest essay, will demonstrate how nature and the cosmic solitudes can loom over the most casual incident. Consider a tiny poem called "Valley Candle," scarcely needing explication if read attentively:

> My candle burned alone in an immense valley.
> Beams of the huge night converged upon it,
> Until the wind blew.
> Then beams of the huge night
> Converged upon its image,
> Until the wind blew. [39]

The little human light, seemingly pulling the night to itself or pushing it back, shrinks as the wind blows it out; and then the memory of its shining shrinks in turn as the night wind blows—and then?

So, too, "The Curtains in the House of the Metaphysician," at first drifting pleasantly in the summer air, are then touched by the "ponderous deflations of distance," the winds, or the cloud movements, the sun's dropping from sight, the "silence, wide sleep and solitude/ Of night" until the firmament itself "bares/ The last largeness, bold to see"; and the metaphysician's retreat is open to the

---

[38] Stevens, "The Figure of Youth," *The Necessary Angel*, p. 59.
[39] Stevens, "Valley Candle," *Collected Poems*, p. 51.

remoteness of all space.[40] Emily Dickinson's boldest note is here enlarged, depersonalized, and made masculine.

Try "The Snow Man," in which the reader is asked to become what the snow man is, not human, without the human comforts, without imagination of cold or warmth, without images of winter, dead leaves, or cold—that which *is* as snow man, not at all zero, but perhaps what is between sun and stars.[41] Consider "The Brave Man," the sun, advancing as shadows flee from woods and grass, as stars run away, as human night-fears subside and seem foolish, the brave man, who "Comes up/ From below and walks without meditation." [42] This it is to be truly brave, to walk without fictions, illusions, distortions of reality.

Stevens, then, in his own way confronts nature, its apartness and its nearness, camping on the frontiers of thought with an almost intimidating intrepidity. He knows, of course, that man cannot live in this rare atmosphere; for example, in "Wild Ducks, People and Distances" he admits that we do not swim in permanent wildness, nor yet endure the cold spaces beyond the sky, but turn with gratitude to our villages and their chimneys, our shelters, putting them between us and these "final, fatal distances" beyond.[43] Nor does Stevens evade the age-old problems of evil and death, for in his "Esthetique du Mal" he endeavors to make them serve esthetic ends; yet holding still that

> The greatest poverty is not to live
> In a physical world. [44]

Does it not seem, then, that here is an American poet demanding inclusion in our theme, at once an original poet and one in the American stream of reliance on experience and the nature about

---

[40] Stevens, "The Curtains in the House of the Metaphysician," *ibid.*, p. 62.
[41] Stevens, "The Snow Man," *ibid.*, p. 9.
[42] Stevens, "The Brave Man," *ibid.*, p. 138.
[43] Stevens, "Wild Ducks," *ibid.*, p. 328.
[44] Stevens, "Esthetique du Mal," *ibid.*, pp. 313–326, quotation from p. 325.

him for his vision of reality? Whitman, tired of the figures and the charts of the "learn'd astronomer," wandered away by himself "And from time to time/ Look'd up in perfect silence at the stars." Stevens, whose mind tired much less easily before figures or stars, was a student, an epistemologist of sorts, a modern man. Emerson pressed too eagerly from nature to idealism, rejecting the past in his reliance on self and the present. Stevens, armed with more modern tools, said bluntly that the poet's ambition must be "to press away from mysticism toward that ultimate good sense which we term civilization." [45] Yet, looking more closely, we see in Stevens the same impulse to push poetry and philosophy to their base in concreteness, to wrest what can be known from the data which our senses may gather. One wonders how much Stevens knew of modern studies in anthropology, semantics, mythologies, the science of man. Certainly it was enough to give him support in his rejection of the familiar answers.

Wallace Stevens may well be seen, it appears, as a kind of culmination of an American strain, the ultimate in a rigorous insistence that we must go directly to the primal experience, that man is one with his universe, not apart from it, and that the ultimate reality is in the blend of the reality that envelops all and the imagination of man that constructs and affirms from that data. [46]

[45] Stevens, "Effects of Analogy," *The Necessary Angel*, p. 116.

[46] Since writing this last sentence, I find in Roy Harvey Pearce's book, *The Continuity of American Poetry* (page 404), the statement that Stevens' work is "the culminating position . . . in the continuity of the antinomian strain of American poetry." Corroborative, too, is an essay by Joseph N. Riddel, "Wallace Stevens' 'Visibility of Thought'" *PMLA*, LXXVII (September, 1962), 482–498.

xv. Epilogue

WE HAVE COME a fair distance in our exploration of what an original, untamed nature in a New World and the experience of men isolated upon its shores may have contributed to the formation of something vaguely to be labelled the American mind, the American way, the native strain in American literature. We have moved from the first Elizabethan Englishmen on these shores through the Revolution and the first concerns of young writers seeking native similes and metaphors to a Wallace Stevens, refusing finally, in the name of nature, the authority of similes themselves.

Have we, like Stevens' man with the blue guitar, composed a tune in danger of being more fiction than reality? Has some chauvinistic impulse colored the threads in the weaving? Much good paper and florid rhetoric has been expended on such generalities as "the American way," and "what it is to be American." Such labors, it may well be, are doomed to futility and obfuscation, increasingly so as Europe becomes more Americanized and America becomes ever more entangled in the sorry old pattern of recurring crises.

Yet we have not insisted at any point on a total separateness. The

American debt to the past is obvious, and the more easily defended, if one were forced to pretend an issue. Nevertheless, the American colonies and states from the beginning, and whatever the reasons— and one reason, surely, was the revolt from European paternalism —have carried the connotations of a greater-than-ordinary freedom. British institutions were themselves the freest of those in the Europe which the colonists had left. Further, authority at a distance is never easy to enforce, and new occasions imposed autonomy, whether intended or not. Pertinent also, the political struggles in England in the seventeenth century had concluded in an affirmation of British "rights" and the larger philosophy of the natural rights of man, powerful factors both in the American revolutionary sentiment. Still further, the American colonies had no feudal system to shed, no titled nobility, no ecclesiastical centralization, no enforceable restrictions on free land or the westward push, no large Indian population to oppose a serious resistance, no observable hindrance on a rising individualism. In short, the stage was set from the start for an unusual degree of individual autonomy, the reference of the individual to his own and the common experience.

Travellers in North America commented often on these surface phenomena, the individualism, the resourcefulness and the lawlessness, and the solitudes risked on the far-flung frontier. They have continued to do so into the twentieth century. Rupert Brooke, British poet, crossing the Canadian Rockies early in the century, observed that these austere peaks and valleys could never have known, could never know, the European softening by legends of fairies, trolls, elves, even of human presences. Always they must remain as if each viewer saw them for the first time and left them as he saw them in their solitary remoteness. John Cowper Powys, British novelist, attempting to identify his impressions, wrote: "The essential spirit of America . . . is a psychic quality immediately associated with the geography of the continent. . . . Between this landscape and this character a psychic reciprocity . . . older than any science." [1] And W. H. Auden, more recently prefacing an anthology of American poets, found the most characteristic note among Americans to be an intimacy with a lonely nature. The Americans, he said, can still imagine nature without man, and man without civilized trappings or traditions, and can still, he implies, like it that way.[2]

However fanciful some of these *aperçus* may appear, who can think them totally so? Where in European literature shall we duplicate a Thoreau, a Whitman, a Mark Twain, a Hemingway, a Robert Frost, a Robinson Jeffers, a Wallace Stevens? None of these is to be judged wholly by European criteria. They are ours not by chauvinism, but by our response to something in ourselves as in them. The European may apply to them his own accustomed yardsticks; but the connotations are his and are not the same, nor are we compelled to defend a foreign standard.

There may be, then, something to the American pretension that he retains somewhat more flexibility within his customs, somewhat less of respect for the traditional absolutes than does his European cousin, and that he prefers it that way. Europeans, it appears, do still show more respect for intellectualized systems of thought, are better informed in the use of such specialized vocabulary, do value more steadily formalized codes of manners, logic, and tradition, and do attach to the American's relative indifference the stigma of social ineptness. Americans do, perhaps, gravitate somewhat more readily toward the pragmatic, respecting experience over theoretical formulae, do retain a somewhat larger confidence in the human potential, under opportunity and encouragement. When Harvard's ex-presi-

[1] John Cowper Powys, "The American Scene and Character," *Century Magazine,* 115 (December, 1927), 176–184, quotation from p. 179.

[2] W. H. Auden (ed.), *The Criterion Book of Modern American Verse.* "There is indeed [says Auden, Introduction, p. 16] an American mentality which is new and unique in the world but it is the product less of conscious political action than of nature, and the new and unique environment of the American continent."

dent, James B. Conant, after four years in Europe, reports [3] that the American way in science is more truly the "empirical inductive" as compared to the European's "theoretical deductive," and further that the American habit is carried over more often into law, education, political science, and perhaps even, hopefully, into human affairs and the future of nations, we tend to respond with a curious compound of intellectual and preferential agreement. Even in the effort of a Camus or a Malraux to recover something of human dignity for the individual—Camus's argument, for example, that the crime of Europe is that adhesion to ideologies which condemns men to death for being stubbornly human and not ideologically patterned—even here we read a groping for an American principle and wonder why Camus did not cite the American Revolution in his *L'Homme Revolté* (*The Rebel*) as an illustration of his central plea for "rebellion" against what belittles man as over "revolution," which makes men their own self-condemning judges in the name of some arbitrary and largely theoretical "system."

Yet having said so much, we immediately recall the vast reservoirs of obscurantism in America, the persistent temptations to demagoguery and facile panaceas in the name of popular and unthinking sentiment, and realize that the rosier picture lies as much in the hope as in the practice. It lies, too, in the best effort and exercise of the American mind, which refuses to surrender the hope or to exchange it for a doubtful reliance on force masking as philosophy.

Being American may connote a relative egalitarianism despite the abuses of great wealth, as well as a good will and enthusiasm along with an easy vulgarity and commonplaceness of taste. It also connotes spaciousness, the ready hospitality of a people not too crowded, a relative lessening of the harsher edges of social superiorities. At any rate, the American carries still this sort of vision of himself, with

---

[3] James B. Conant, "The Advancement of Knowledge in the United States in the Nineteenth Century," *Colorado Quarterly*, XI (Winter, 1963), 229–244.

overtones of the frontier past within it; and whereas the Englishman equates freedom with the open seas and the privacy of his
home, the American measures his in terms of large open spaces. No
one, not even Henry James, has ever written of Europe in the same
terms. The charm of England or France, for Americans, has been
that of a cosier intimacy of setting, the homestead hallowed by
legend, but not that native spaciousness which dilates the heart and
spells the very breath of freedom.

There will never again be such a frontier as ours. All is against it:
the end of a great age of terrestrial exploration, speeded transportation, exploding populations, governmental controls. It may well be
that the hard hand of historical necessity will rob us in turn of that
uniqueness, and with it the dream of an open society. Shall we therefore become prematurely jubilant over that loss? Merle Curti, in his
Probing Our Past (1955), observes that if by 1984 our institutions
shall have crystallized, we shall henceforth know no further exploration of the meaning of democracy. One insistence within any definition of that word must be, that is, the freedom to redefine its meaning
whenever the need arises, yet so as to preserve its central guarantees
for the human being within it. This task our poets and novelists may
continue, not by any command or any didacticism, but simply by
the perpetual freedom of art.

There is a certain sullenness in the faces of democracy today, a
kind of subdued truculence, as of men whose expectations have been
defeated. Elsewhere vicious men have stolen the good words for
their own nefarious purposes. Language is prostituted until no one
places confidence in what is said. Automation will do the plowing
and the reaping, break the new trails, wipe out the enemies. The
simple man seems expendable, deprived of a central role, insignificant. What is lacking must lie, then, within the human spectrum
and the individual's position in a world which belittles him more and
more. The frontiers today are of a vast and cosmic sort, touching all
continents and reaching beyond them into space. Perhaps there man

will recover something of a lost dignity, though it seems hardly likely that so single a mechanical triumph alone can touch the heart of the matter.

Nevertheless, new frontiers force new similes and metaphors, which draw as always on the new experience for which the old words are not quite adequate. The poets have still work to do. The earth itself shrinks, becomes a frail item in great spaces, the metaphor for a new concept of man and his meaning. Appropriate, then, to this interim period is another American poem, one which starts once more in old Europe, looks again beyond it to the western Pacific, yet launches beyond it not, as in Whitman, to India, but into the prophetic spaces. It is by Robinson Jeffers:

The Eye

The Atlantic is a stormy moat; and the Mediterranean,
The blue pool in the old garden,
More than five thousand years has drunk sacrifice
Of ships and blood, and shines in the sun; but here the Pacific—
Our ships, planes, wars are perfectly irrelevant.
Neither our present blood-feud with the brave dwarfs
Nor any future world-quarrel of westering
And eastering man, the bloody migrations, greed of power,
        clash of faiths—
Is a speck of dust on the great scale-pan.
Here from this mountain shore, headland beyond stormy headland
        plunging like dolphins through the blue sea-smoke
Into pale sea—look west at the hill of water: it is half
        the planet: this dome, this half-globe, this bulging
Eyeball of water, arched over to Asia,
Australia and white Antarctica: those are the eyelids that
        never close; this is the staring unsleeping
Eye of the earth, and what it watches is not our wars. [4]

---

[4] Robinson Jeffers, "The Eye," *The Double Axe*, p. 126.

BIBLIOGRAPHY

This bibliography makes no pretense to being complete, but is merely an acknowledgment of the primary sources cited within the text, and of secondary titles mentioned or, in some cases, recommended as useful.

PRIMARY SOURCES

American Culture Series, 1493–1875. Microfilm. A useful selection of early Americana. Ann Arbor, Michigan: University Microfilms, 1953–1963.

Beverly, Robert. *History and Present State of Virginia, 1755.* Edited by L. B. Wright. Chapel Hill: University of North Carolina Press, 1947.

Bradford, William. *Of Plimouth Plantation.* Edited by S. E. Morison. New York: Alfred A. Knopf, Inc. 1952.

Brown, Charles Brockden. *Edgar Huntley.* Boston, 1827.

Clemens, Samuel L. *Roughing It.* Chicago: F. G. Gilman, 1874.

Clough, Wilson O. "Not from Landscape, Not from Flight," *Symposium,* I (Spring, 1962), 15–19.

———. "The Cult of the Bad Man of the West," *Texas Quarterly,* V (Autumn, 1962), 311–320.

———. "Wyoming and the Westward Movement," *American Journal of Sociology,* XXXV (1930), 808–815.

Cooper, James Fenimore. *Works.* New York: P. F. Collier, 1891.

Crane, Stephen. *Collected Poems.* New York: Alfred A. Knopf, Inc., 1951.

———. *Twenty Stories.* New York: Alfred A. Knopf, Inc., 1940.

Dimsdale, Thomas J. *Vigilantes of Montana.* Norman: University of Oklahoma Press, 1953.

Dwight, Timothy. *Travels in New-England and New-York* [sic]. London, 1823.

Early American Imprints, 1639–1800. Edited by Clifton K. Shipton. Worcester, Massachusetts: American Antiquarian Society, 1955– .

Edwards, Jonathan. *Representative Selections from Jonathan Edwards.* Edited by Clarence H. Fause and Thomas H. Johnson. New York: American Book Company, 1935.

Emerson, Ralph Waldo. *Works.* Boston: Houghton Mifflin Company, 1883.

Faulkner, William. *Go Down, Moses.* New York: Random House, Inc., 1942.

Ferril, Thomas Hornsby. *New and Selected Poems.* New York: Harper Brothers, 1952.

Filson, John. *The Discovery, Settlement, and Present State of Kentucke.* Facsimile. Edited by W. R. Jilson. Louisville, Kentucky: Morton and Company, 1930.

Frost, Robert. *Complete Poems of Robert Frost.* New York: Holt, Rinehart and Winston, Inc., 1949.

——. *In the Clearing.* New York: Holt, Rinehart and Winston, Inc., 1962.

Griswold, Rufus W. *The Female Poets of America.* Philadelphia: Carey and Hart, 1849.

Hall, Clayton C. (ed.). *Narratives of Early Maryland.* New York: Charles Scribner's Sons, 1910.

Hawthorne, Nathaniel. *Complete Works.* Boston: Houghton Mifflin Company, 1882.

James, Henry. *The American.* New York: Charles Scribner's Sons, 1907.

——. *Hawthorne.* New York: Harper Brothers, 1879.

Jeffers, Robinson. *Roan Stallion, Tamar, and Other Poems.* New York: Random House, Inc., 1934.

——. *The Selected Poetry of Robinson Jeffers.* New York: Random House, Inc., 1938.

——. *The Double Axe and Other Poems.* New York: Random House, Inc., 1948.

Jefferson, Thomas. *Notes on the State of Virginia.* Edited by W. M. Peden. Chapel Hill: University of North Carolina Press, 1954.

Mayhew, Jonathan. *Seven Sermons.* Boston, 1748. Reproduced in Early American Imprints.

Melville, Herman. *Israel Potter.* New York: Albert & Charles Boni, Inc., 1924.

——. *Moby-Dick.* Edited by Wilbur Thorp. New York: Oxford University Press, 1947.

——. *White-Jacket.* London: Oxford University Press, 1929.

Neihardt, John G. *A Cycle of the West.* New York: Macmillan Company, 1949.

Norris, Frank. *The Octopus.* Boston: Houghton Mifflin Company, 1958.

Robinson, Edwin Arlington. *Collected Poems.* New York: Macmillan Company, 1929.

Rush, Benjamin. *Essays, Literary, Moral and Philosophical.* 2d ed. Philadelphia, 1806. Microfilmed in American Culture Series.

Ruxton, George Frederick. *Ruxton of the Rockies.* Edited by LeRoy R. Hafen. Norman: University of Oklahoma Press, 1950.

Sandburg, Carl. *Complete Poems*. New York: Harcourt, Brace and Company, Inc., 1950.

Shipton, Clifton K. (ed.). *Early American Imprints, 1639–1800*. Worcester, Massachusetts: American Antiquarian Society, 1955– .

Steinbeck, John. *The Long Valley*. New York: Viking Press, Inc., 1938.

Stevens, Wallace. *Collected Poems of Wallace Stevens*. New York: Alfred A. Knopf, Inc., 1957.

———. *Opus Posthumous*. New York: Alfred A. Knopf, Inc., 1957.

———. *The Necessary Angel*. New York: Alfred A. Knopf, Inc., 1951.

Tate, Allen. *Collected Essays*. Denver: Alan Swallow, Publisher, 1959.

Thoreau, Henry David. *Writings of Henry Thoreau*. Boston: Houghton Mifflin Company, 1893.

Tocqueville, Alexis de. *Democracy in America*. Edited by Phillips Bradley. New York: Alfred A. Knopf, Inc. (Vintage Books), 1954.

Trollope, Frances. *Domestic Manners of the Americans*. New York: Dodd, Mead & Company, Inc., 1927.

Whitman, Walt. *Complete Poetry and Selected Prose*. Edited by James E. Miller, Jr. New York: Houghton Mifflin Company (paperback), 1960.

———. *Complete Prose Works*. Boston: Small, 1901.

———. *Leaves of Grass*. Edited by Emory Holloway. Garden City, New York: Doubleday, Page and Company, 1929.

Wise, John. *Vindication of the Government of New England Churches*. Boston, 1717. Reproduced in Early American Imprints.

Wolfe, Thomas. *From Death to Morning*. New York: Charles Scribner's Sons, 1935.

———. *Of Time and the River*. New York: Charles Scribner's Sons, 1935.

Wright, Solomon A. *My Rambles as East Texas Cowboy, Hunter, Fisherman, Tie Cutter*. Austin, Texas: Texas Folklore Society, 1942.

SECONDARY SOURCES

Auden, W. H. (ed.). *The Criterion Book of Modern American Verse*. New York: Criterion Books, 1956.

Beach, Joseph W. *American Fiction, 1920–1940*. New York: Macmillan Company, 1941.

Botkin, Benjamin A. *A Treasury of Western Folklore*. New York: Crown Publishers, Inc., 1944.

Burt, Struthers. *The Delectable Mountains*. New York: Charles Scribner's Sons, 1927.

Canby, H. S. *Turn West, Turn East*. Boston: Houghton Mifflin Company, 1951.

Chase, Richard. *The American Novel and its Tradition*. Garden City, New York: Doubleday & Company, Inc. (Anchor Books), 1957.

Clark, H. H. (ed.). *Major American Poets*. New York: American Book Company, 1936.

———— (ed.). *Transitions in American Literary History*. Durham, North Carolina: Duke University Press, 1954.

Clough, Wilson O. (ed.). *Intellectual Origins of American National Thought: Pages from the Books the Founding Fathers Read*. New York: Citadel Press (paperback), 1961.

Conant, James B. "The Advancement of Knowledge in the United States in the Nineteenth Century," *Colorado Quarterly*, XI (Winter, 1963), 229–244.

Cowie, Alexander. *The Rise of the American Novel*. New York: American Book Company, 1948.

Cowley, Malcolm. "Naturalism in American Literature," reprinted in *Evolutionary Thought in America*. Edited by Stow Persons. New York: George Braziller, 1956.

Curti, Merle. *The Growth of American Thought*. New York: Harper Brothers, 1943.

De Voto, Bernard. *Mark Twain's America*. Boston: Little, Brown & Company, 1932.

————. *The Course of Empire*. Boston: Houghton Mifflin Company, 1952.

Emerich, Duncan. *It's an Old Wild West Custom*. New York: Vanguard Press, Inc., 1949.

Fause, Clarence H., and Thomas H. Johnson (eds.). *Representative Selections from Jonathan Edwards*. New York: American Book Company, 1935.

Feidelson, Charles, Jr. *Symbolism and American Literature*. Chicago: University of Chicago Press, 1953.

Ferril, Thomas Hornsby. "Writing in the Rockies," *The Rocky Mountain Reader*. Edited by Ray B. West. New York: E. P. Dutton & Company, Inc., 1945.

Foerster, Norman. *American Poetry and Prose*. 4th ed. New York: Houghton Mifflin Company, 1957.

————. *Nature in American Literature*. New York: Russell Sage Foundation, 1958.

Gabriel, Ralph H. *The Course of American Democratic Thought*. New York: Ronald Press Company, 1940.

Geismar, Maxwell. *Writers in Crisis*. Boston: Houghton Mifflin Company, 1942.

Haley, J. Evetts. *Charles Goodnight, Cowman and Plainsman*. Norman: University of Oklahoma Press, 1950.

Hazard, L. L. *The Frontier in American Literature*. Chicago: Cornwell Company, 1927.

Horton, R. W., and H. W. Edwards. *Backgrounds of American Literary Thought*. New York: Appleton-Century-Crofts, Inc., 1952.

House, Boyce. *Cowtown Columnist*. San Antonio, Texas: Naylor Press, 1946.

Howard, Robert W. *This is the West*. New York: New American Library (Signet Books), 1957.

Jones, Howard Mumford. *Ideas in America*. Cambridge, Massachusetts: Harvard University Press, 1944.

Kouwenhoven, John A. *Made in America*. Boston: Charles T. Branford Company, 1957.

Lawrence, D. H. *Studies in Classic American Literature*. New York: Seltzer, 1923.

Lewis, R. W. B. *The American Adam*. Chicago: University of Chicago Press, 1955.

———. "The Hero in the New World: William Faulkner's 'The Bear'," *Kenyon Review*, 13 (Autumn, 1951), 641–660.

Matthiessen, F. O. *The American Renaissance*. New York: Oxford University Press, 1941.

Miller, Perry. *Errand into the Wilderness*. Cambridge, Massachusetts: Harvard University Press, 1956.

———. *Jonathan Edwards*. New York: William Sloane Associates, 1949.

———. *The Raven and the Whale*. New York: Harcourt, Brace and Company, Inc., 1956.

———, and Thomas H. Johnson. *The Puritans*. New York: American Book Company, 1938.

Parrington, Vernon L. *Main Currents in American Thought*. 3 vols. New York: Harcourt Brace and Company, 1927–1930.

Pearce, Roy Harvey. *The Continuity of American Poetry*. Princeton, New Jersey: Princeton University Press, 1961.

Persons, Stow (ed.). *Evolutionary Thought in America*. New York: George Braziller, 1956.

Powys, John Cowper. "The American Scene and Character," *Century Magazine*, 115 (December, 1927), 176–184.

Priestley, J. B. *Midnight on the Desert*. New York: Harper Brothers, 1937.

Riddel, Joseph N. "Wallace Stevens' 'Visibility of Thought'," *PMLA*, LXXVII (September, 1962), 482–498.

Rourke, Constance. *The Roots of American Culture*. New York: Harcourt, Brace and Company, Inc., 1942.

Santayana, George. *Character and Opinion in the United States*. New York: Charles Scribner's Sons, 1921.

Smith, Henry Nash. *Virgin Land*. Cambridge, Massachusetts: Harvard University Press, 1950.

Spencer, Benjamin T. *The Quest for Nationality*. Syracuse: Syracuse University Press, 1957.

Spiller, Robert E. *The Cycle of American Literature*. New York: Macmillan Company, 1955.

———, *et al.* (eds.). *Literary History of the United States.* 3 vols. New York: Macmillan Company, 1948.

Sweet, William W. *Religion in the Development of American Culture, 1765–1840.* New York: Charles Scribner's Sons, 1952.

Turner, Frederick Jackson. *The Frontier in American History.* New York: Henry Holt and Company, Inc., 1920.

Warshow, Robert. "Movie Chronicle: The Westerner," *Partisan Review,* XXI (March, 1954), 235–238.

West, Ray B. (ed.). *The Rocky Mountain Reader.* New York: E. P. Dutton & Company, Inc., 1947.

Williams, William Carlos. "Against the Weather," *Selected Essays.* New York: Random House, Inc., 1954.

Willison, George F. *Saints and Sinners.* New York: Raynal and Hitchcock, 1945.

Wilson, Edmund. "Books," *New Yorker,* XXI (May 26, 1945), 75–77.

Winters, Yvor. *Maule's Curse.* Norfolk, Connecticut: New Directions, 1950.

Wright, L. B. *Culture on the Moving Frontier.* Bloomington: Indiana University Press, 1955.

INDEX

symbol: birth of, 78–79; frontier as, 78,
82, 84, 144–145, 151; for Emerson,
101, 104, 105; for Whitman, 137–139;
status symbol, 160; from experience,
185. SEE ALSO metaphor

taciturnity: on frontier, 15, 50–51, 62
Tahiti: 126
Tate, Alan: 117–119, 124
Taylor, Bayard: 173
Tennessee: 170
tension: as base for literature: 117–119,
124; in Hawthorne, 117–119; the
west as escape from, 157, 159; in
Faulkner, 183
Texas: 66, 71, 133; legend of, 43–44, 46
Texas Folklore Society: 50
"Thanatopsis": 63, 64
theme: of this book, 10–16 passim, 183;
native, 59, 84, 132, 147; frontier as,
73–74, 77–87 passim; in Hawthorne,
119–125 passim. SEE ALSO frontier
theocracy: waning, 38, 89; in Edwards,
94
theology: traditional, 78, 89; in Edwards,
81. SEE ALSO religion
This is the West: 44
Thompson, Ben: 44–45
Thoreau, Henry: 62, 83, 110–115
passim, 118, 119, 121, 183, 191, 208;
as American, 15, 29, 108; and the
state, 29, 130; and Indian, 77, 78,
114; and reality, 77–78, 111, 112;
and westward pull, 99; and past, 99–
100, 111; and creative act, 111; and
economics, 111; and experience, 111;
and innocence, 111; nature in, 110–
115 passim; individualism in, 111,
112, 115; cosmic in, 111, 114; and
society, 111–115 passim; solitude in,
111, 114, 116; style in, 111, 134;
Puritan in, 112; independency in, 112,
115; simplicity, 112; didacticism in,
113; humor in, 115; and Melville,
128; and Frost, 186; and Jeffers, 192,
196; and Stevens, 198, 200, 202
thought. SEE frontiers of thought

Tocqueville, Alexis de: on American
independency, 34; on American appeal
to experience, 83, 89, 129; on America
as new fact, 86; on American solitude,
117
tolerance: in eighteenth century, 103; in
Emerson, 110; on frontier, 89–90
Tolstoi, Aleksei: 173
tourist: in west, 42, 43, 56–57, 73, 133,
136, 147
Track of the Cat: 151
tradition: of Old World, 16, 29; American rejection of, 29, 35, 83, 88, 89,
106, 107, 162; absence of, 29, 144,
207, 208; absence of, in Hawthorne,
120; absence of, in Whitman, 134,
139; values of, 82; sources of, 86; in
language, 16, 92, 108; probed in
literature, 117–119; in west, 159
tragedy: in Hawthorne, 120; in literature, 167
transcendentalism: and frontier, 82;
sources of, 82 n.; German, 82 n., 107;
in religion, 88, 91; Lockean base of,
103, 104, 105; in Emerson, 107; solitude in, 116, 120; in Whitman, 124,
184; in Frost, 186, 191; in Robinson,
187, 191; in Jeffers, 196; in Stevens,
197
Treasury of Western Folklore: 46–47
Trollope, Frances: 34–35
Twain, Mark: 128, 208; as American
spokesman, 10, 16; pull of west in,
99, 163; code of, 163; pessimism, 167;
and Faulkner, 183
Turgenev, Ivan: 173
Turn West, Turn East: 163
Turner, Frederick J.: thesis of, 41, 91–
92, 183

Unitarian: 96; Emerson as, 102
universe: order in, 35, 103, 104, 105,
172; eighteenth-century view of, 103;
scheme of, 114
urban society: in literature, 102; in
America, 152
Uses of the Past: 19

JUN 24 1965 R

Aug 1...

PS163 C6
+The necessary ea+Clough, Wilson O

0 00 02 0197605 7
MIDDLEBURY COLLEGE